A Wonderful
Little Girl

A Wonderful
Little Girl

*Starving for fame: how Sarah Jacobs
bewitched the world*

SIÂN BUSBY

 SHORT BOOKS

First published in 2004 by
Short Books
15 Highbury Terrace
London N5 1UP

10 9 8 7 6 5 4 3 2 1

A CIP catalogue record for this book
is available from the British Library.

ISBN 1-904095-70-4

Printed in Great Britain by
Bookmarque Ltd, Croydon

For Nana, still missed

SARAH JACOB

19th February 1869
To the Editor of the Welshman

A STRANGE CASE

*SIR, – Allow me to invite the attention of your
readers to a most extraordinary case. Sarah Jacob, a
little girl of twelve years of age and daughter of Mr
Evan Jacob, Lletherneuadd, in this parish, has not
partaken of a single grain of food whatever during
the last sixteen months. She did occasionally swallow
a few drops of water during the first few months of
this period; but now she does not even do that. She
still looks pretty well in the face, and continues in
the possession of all her mental faculties. She is in
this, and several other respects, a wonderful little
girl.*

Medical men persist in saying that the thing is

quite impossible, but all the nearest neighbours, who are thoroughly acquainted with the circumstances of the case, entertain no doubt whatever on the subject, and

I am myself of the same opinion. Would it not be worth their while for medical men to make an investigation into the nature of this strange case? Mr Evan Jacob would readily admit into his house any respectable person, who might be anxious to watch it, and see for himself.

I might add that Lletherneuadd is a farm-house, about a mile from New Inn, in this parish.

Yours Faithfully,
Rev. Evan Jones, BD
THE VICAR OF LLANFIHANGEL-AR-ARTH

21ST DECEMBER 1869, LLETHERNEUADD

The little girl's corpse was small – not above four feet five inches – yet it was well developed. The armpits and pubes, it was noted, showed precocious puberty. The child's famed beauty was still apparent, even four days after death: the plump cheeks tinged with a pink blush; the long, delicate fingers; the handsome, well formed head covered with an abundance of black hair. She resembled some heroine from an ancient Celtic tale. The large dark eyes, however, though still thickly lashed, had lost their once-famed glittering brilliance and now stared out, harrowed, sunk deep in their sockets, ringed with dark, dark circles. Only the eyes betrayed how much she must have suffered at the end of her little life.

The two surgeons had to work quickly against the light, now fast fading into the impenetrable gloom of a Welsh winter twilight. They moved noiselessly, intent upon the neat little body laid out before them, pausing only to slop their hands in the basin of reddening water, or drop their spent instruments into the felt-lined trays. The soft, plump flesh yielded nearly all its secrets to their scalpels and probing: a beautifully developed brain beneath the skull; lungs and a heart that were healthy and free from any trace of disease. Most revealingly of all, the surgeons discovered a thick layer of fat, about half an inch over the upper chest and up to one inch on the lower part of the abdomen. Their fingers forced open the small mouth with its perfect white teeth, and slipped down the empty throat. In all of this, they were watched over with rapt attention by a small group of medical gentlemen, every one of whom had good reason to be there; reasons that went beyond mere curiosity. One of them would later remark that the child's body had the appearance of a freshly slaughtered animal.

It took the doctors barely an hour to determine that there was no deformity of limb or organs and none of the symptoms of tuberculosis, beri-beri or meningitis – in short, no trace of any disease or injury that might have caused the death of an otherwise healthy, normally developed, twelve-year-old girl.

The body, they confirmed, did not have so much as a bedsore upon it. Nor did they discover any sign of emaciation. True, the bladder was completely empty, but in the gut was half a pound of hardened excrement, which may have been there for a fortnight – perhaps even longer. This they handed over as evidence to the attending police sergeant. Later, one of the medical men, in the interest of science, was able to examine it under a microscope, where he discerned traces of some cereal foodstuff along with the bones of either a small fish or bird.

By three o'clock the light was almost gone, but there was just time for two more intriguing observations to be made. Firstly, the child's toenails had been cut perhaps a week before death, and under the nail of the big toe on the right foot there was a dark indentation as if something had pinched it. It was not for the physicians to draw conclusions, merely to present their findings, but one of them wondered whether this had occurred as a result of the clipping or by some other means. Had the girl attempted to use her toe in order, for example, to prise a cork from a bottle?

Secondly and of more obvious significance, the right shoulder was more prominent than the left and the left armpit was quite hollow. 'Sufficiently so', the senior surgeon Mr John Phillips opined, 'to contain a half-pint bottle if it were put into it.'

The examination complete, the child's body was prepared for the visit of the coroner and jurors. In accordance with the law of the time, they were required to view it *in situ* before the inquest could commence. Then it could be returned to the family for a Christian burial. At eleven o'clock on the bleak morning of Wednesday 22nd December 1869, the little Welsh Fasting Girl was laid out for the last time in the humble back parlour where she had died and where for nine months she had been the object of curiosity and celebrity. And where she now received her last visitors.

***

Looking back on it when writing his memoirs in 1894, the Reverend Evan Jones blamed the train for everything. Before the train had come hurtling through Pencader station, with its great maw of hellish fire and its billowing clouds of acrid smoke, Wales had been an innocent and gentle place. The train's demented screeching had shattered the silence of the valleys; its soot and muck had besmirched and sullied the skies above; its tracks had twisted their way over the mountain and ripped open the ancient soil beneath. The Carmarthen & Cardigan Railway Company had brought modernity; but it had also brought Irish navvies and Brummie station-masters; cargo-loads of strangers to gawp and gape; unbelievers and doubters. In the end, the train brought the news of Sarah Jacob's death down the line and across the Epynt range, the Cambrians, the Brecon Beacons, the Black Mountains, and out into that other land beyond.

By then she had become so famous that it was enough for newspaper billboards in London to proclaim simply 'The Welsh Fasting Girl is Dead'. For three days before every newsroom in the land had pullulated with rumour. In the edition of the *Cambrian Times* prepared on the Friday as she lay dying, the editor confessed to his readers that he was 'hoping for the best, while at the same time fearing the worst'.

When the waiting was over and the worst had been realised, the headline in most of the British press (and some of the Continental and American papers, too) was the same – 'The Welsh Fasting Girl is Dead'. The *Illustrated London News* devoted its entire editorial in the final edition of 1869 to the sad tale of 'the poor little Welsh Fasting Girl'. The more gossipy *Police News* splashed two successive editions with artists' impressions of her last hours and a 'charming view' of Lletherneuadd, its farmyard populated by toffs in top-hats and bustled and bonneted ladies.

The Welsh Fasting Girl was such a sensational story that it took up prime position on the front page, forcing down a number of other dramatic stories: for example, an 'atrocious' attack on a woman by her husband in Ewell. In the Christmas 1869 edition of *All the Year Round*, Charles Dickens, ever in tune with the popular imagination, ruminated upon the power of 'weak and emaciated girls' to arouse curiosity and anxiety in equal measure – a phenomenon the creator of Little Dorrit and Little Nell understood all too well.

Over the next few months, the nation's most eminent lawyers pondered the ethical issues the case threw up. Was her death manslaughter, murder or suicide? Sarah Jacob had died, not as a result of any commonplace instance of child abuse and neglect, but in the course of 'a purely scientific inquiry' – sanctioned by no less than eight qualified medical practitioners. Who should stand trial? The parents who apparently stood by and watched their child starve, or the doctors who devised the fatal experiment? Many felt that Science itself should be in the dock.

For its part, the medical establishment placed the blame on Sarah herself, denouncing her as a hysterical girl, the victim of her own personality. Practitioners of the burgeoning science of psychiatry in France, Britain and America scrambled to make their conclusions known and, perhaps too, their reputations.

In his groundbreaking examination of the case, published in 1871, Dr. Robert Fowler forged a link between fasting and 'neurotic' or 'hysterical' behaviour – radical stuff at the time. And when the eminent physician Sir William Gull used the term 'anorexia nervosa' in 1873, he was thinking of the Welsh Fasting Girl, and what her case revealed about the psychology of young women.

Sarah Jacob is sometimes credited with being the first recognised anorexic – she certainly features prominently in modern books on the subject and a university web-site – although there never was any evidence that she deliberately abstained from eating.

And this is the conundrum at the heart of the story. How did a plump and apparently well-nourished child manage to convince large numbers of people – including her parents, vicar and family doctor – that she was a miraculous fasting girl? And what drove her to do it? Her parents persisted in maintaining that she could not eat – even when it was clear that their child was dying. Were they cruel and mendacious, only interested in exploiting her? Or does the evidence point to a quite different conclusion?

The local vicar, Reverend Jones, a man of considerable intellect and ability, was so convinced that Sarah Jacob was miraculous that he risked his reputation and endured months of public scorn in support of her claims. Dr Harries Davies, the family GP, was so sure that the merest offer of food would result in the child's death that he went against all his medical training and professional rationale: instead of forcing Sarah to eat, he stood by and did nothing. And finally, what motivated vast numbers of people to travel huge distances just to see Sarah or touch her hand?

It had only taken a few weeks, once the Reverend Jones's letter had reproduced in all the newspapers, for her to become a major tourist attraction. Throughout the spring and summer of 1869, thousands of people made the arduous journey to the tiny Carmarthenshire farmstead where she languished. In fact, there were soon so many arrivals at Pencader station – which up until then had seen only a daily trickle of dairymen bringing their churns to the milk train – that a profitable refreshments stand was opened.

Under headlines such as 'A Strange Tale from Carmarthenshire' and 'A Visit to see the Wonderful Little Girl', her story occupied the nation every day from March through to December 1869. And not just in the pages of the British popular press: the London *Times*, the *Lancet*, *British Medical Journal* and the American and Continental media all followed the story with fervour. Were all these people victims of some collective delusion – or was there truly something marvellous about the 'wonderful little girl'?

More than 130 years have elapsed since this curious tale unfolded, and the Welsh Fasting Girl still remains an enigma. Sarah Jacob was, by all accounts, a highly intelligent, affectionate, adored, deeply religious and beautiful child. She was also wilful, manipulative, disturbing and disturbed. There are only a few recorded instances of her own words, and in none of them does she reveal her motives. She remained resolute, inscrutable and silent to her last breath; not once did she ask for help or relief. But then troubled children rarely do.

Sarah was a simple peasant girl, who transcended the limitations of her humble destiny, posing such a challenge to reason itself that serious men of science were compelled to destroy her in order to defeat superstition once and for all. She was a saint, a potent symbol of the ineluctable mystery at the heart of life, who within days of her death was recast as an innocent pawn in the battle between Faith and Science, a martyr to Welsh nationalist pride. She was a miracle: a child who starved herself to death.

❦

LLANVIHANGEL-AR-ARTH, *or* YEROTH
(LLAN-FIHANGEL-AR-ARTH), a parish, in the union of
NEWCASTLE-EMLYN, higher division of the hundred of
CATHINOG, county of CARMARTHEN, SOUTH WALES, 12
miles (N. by E.) from Carmarthen; containing 1993
inhabitants... The parish is
pleasantly situated on the river Teivy, over which the
turnpike-road is continued by means of a handsome
stone bridge.

The surrounding scenery is pleasantly diversified,
and in some parts highly picturesque; and the soil,
though varying in different parts, is in general
fertile... The church, dedicated to St. Michael, is
situated on an eminence on the southern bank of the
Teivy... The chapel of Pencader has been in ruins for
nearly a century, but the cemetery is still entire. There
are places of worship for Calvinistic Methodists,
Baptists, and Independents. D. Jones, Esq. pays a mas-
ter £5 per annum for teaching poor children to read
Welsh in a school for more than 120 children... Three
other day schools are carried on, in which 80 boys and
35 girls are educated at the expense of their parents;
and five Sunday schools...

[*From* A Topographical Dictionary of Wales
(S. Lewis, 1844).]

Carmarthenshire in the mid-nineteenth century was, like much of Wales, a poor, backward and forgotten place, inhabited by a people who were for the most part impoverished, down-trodden and utterly isolated from the 'outside world'. But it wasn't always so. Pencader, the nearest town to Sarah's birthplace, Llanfihangel-ar-arth, has a proud history. The name translates as 'The Chieftain's Seat' and a memorial in the town's square nobly asserts that, though 'This nation may be harassed... it can never be weakened. Nor will any other nation than the Welsh or any other language ever answer for this corner of the earth.'

Certainly, in Sarah's time, most people in the area spoke only Welsh. This included Sarah's own family, with the exception of Sarah herself who could read and write in both English and Welsh. Most of the other bilinguists were the professional people, or successful tradesmen of the area – the doctors, priests and teachers of Llanfihangel-ar-arth and Pencader could all speak English, the language of aspiration and education. And they would have been mildly disdainful of the majority of their neighbours – the farmers, weavers, knitters, agricultural labourers – who could, with few exceptions, only speak Welsh.

Pencader was also the centre of fairy activity in Carmarthenshire. In a nearby village, according to an oft-told story, poor Siôn Jenkins had inadvertently stepped into a fairy ring and been transported into the future where he had promptly crumbled to dust. In another enchanted spot closer to the Jacobs' home, many people claimed to have seen the spectral vision of *y Ladi Wen* (the white lady). Spooky tales would have been part of Sarah's daily life. Through the gloomy veil of near-constant rain, the shimmering outline of the corpse candle – eerie harbinger of death – regularly floated by, accompanied by the wind howling down the ravines. Many a shivering soul in the valleys below fancied they could hear the doleful wail of the *cyhyraeth* (hound of death), as plaintive and chilling as the groan of a dying man.

Sarah's village, Llanfihangel-ar-arth, lies just three miles from Pencader on a quiet crossroads. It was tiny in 1869; the entire settlement centred upon its two inns and the area around the church, and consisted of little more than a dozen whitewashed, mud-walled hovels, peeping out mistrustfully from behind their low stone walls and deep hedges. The cottages were strewn about the banks of the three rivers – the Teifi, Tyweli and Talog – which fence the village in; within their boundaries a butcher, village shop, two smithies, two carpenters and a cooper plied their trades to the smallholdings scattered about the valley and the mountainside.

Today the village is merged into Pencader and sits on the fast and busy road from Carmarthen to Cardigan Bay. Its houses are now more numerous and mostly quite modern; but in 1869 the village's inhabitants clung to the hillside, far less sure of their place there than were the dark grey slabs of ancient rock jutting out from thick clumps of moss and heather.

Now it is possible to appreciate the beautiful view of the mountains that surround the village, the peacefulness, and the acre upon acre of lush pasture. But for hundreds of years the rugged mountains hardly tolerated the people who lived below them, a few hardy souls who scraped together just enough from their damp crops and stocking knitting, as had their ancestors, sharing their rudimentary accommodation with sheep as thin as yesterday's broth and a few poor cows.

Well into the twentieth century, these tough people contended with the summers when forage was scarce; laid hay and firewood by for the winter; endured Foot and Mouth disease and the more malignant Rinderpest; fetched water from the river; lived on potatoes, barley bread and buttermilk. They thought nothing of walking several miles in all weathers to the Chapel. It was not an easy way to live.

Lletherneuadd-uchaf, where Sarah was born on 17th June 1857 and where she died on 17th December 1869, is a farm of about 120 acres. It is still there, nestling at the foot of a very steep hill path, which leads down from the village centre. Lletherneuadd translates as 'the house on the slope', but *'llether'*, in the romantic way the Welsh language has of endowing descriptions of the landscape with emotion, also carries the sense of 'overlying', of something smothering and oppressive.

Sarah's parents, Evan and Hannah, must have felt pleased with themselves when they came to the farm, a hopeful young couple with two small daughters, sometime in the 1850s. Back then the holding was a mere thirty acres, but over the course of Sarah's childhood they gradually acquired some of their neighbour's fields. By 1867 they had steadily built up the tenancy until it was one of the biggest in the area – if not in the whole of Wales. They would have kept at least a dozen cows on a farm of this size (not the sixty kept there today) and the resulting milk yield would have been the mainstay of the family income.

The Jacob homestead was a *ty hir*, a small single-storey stone building, with people living at one end and animals at the other, only a small improvement on the ancient cave dwelling from which it had evolved. The stable part of the house was well proportioned and its floor was slightly raised to form a sort of platform.

This was a legacy of the ancient origins of the building, from a time when the Celtic people believed that cattle milked better if they could see the flames of the cottage fire, which protected all from evil and harm. The step divided the stalls from the human accommodation and helped keep the muck at bay.

At some stage in the building's long history, the byre at Lletherneuadd had been separated from the family's quarters by the addition of a simple mud wall, and was accessed through a separate door on the outside of the building. In most other respects, however, the Jacobs' home – and their way of life – would have remained much as it had always been, unchanged for hundreds of years.

Even by the standards of the day, the farm would have felt remote. The family's nearest neighbours were at the mill, Ffynnon-felen, a good half-mile away to the north. Their other neighbours (all farms) were more than a mile's hike across fields. The Independent Chapel at Pencader, where the family worshipped, was three miles away, as was the family doctor, at Llandyssul. The hospital was a fourteen-mile journey along a typically bad Welsh road, impassable when it flooded, which, needless to say, it frequently did.

In such a setting you had to be self-sufficient. It helped if you were tough and industrious, but you also needed to be pragmatic and set your sights low. The boredom and loneliness of the long dark nights and seemingly interminable winters had the power to drive a sensitive and thoughtful person mad.

Sarah's father, Evan Jacob was born in 1830, a few miles north of Pencader in Llandyssul, Cardiganshire, so he was technically a 'Cardi', reputedly a thrifty and cautious people. The only photograph of him, taken at the time of Sarah's death, shows a dark-haired man with a long craggy face, high cheekbones and handsome if rather brooding features set under a heavy brow. His eyes have something ancient about them. Evan was, by all accounts, a hardworking and honest man and a good farmer.

In 1869, the rent on Lletherneuadd stood at £61 per

year – a tidy sum, more than twice the average annual earnings for most of the population – but Evan Jacob always paid his landlords on time and in full. His status as a fifty-guinea farmer earned him the right to vote and, consequently, occupy a respected place in the village hierarchy.

The Jacob family was by no means well off – they had no lavatory; they rarely had fresh meat at their table – but compared with many of their neighbours they were a success story. Evan was deacon of the Independent Chapel at Pencader and an Overseer of the Poor – this last a position of immense trust, under which he was charged with collecting taxes and dispensing clothes, food and fuel to the needy.

Unlike lots of poor farmers of the time, Evan was able to read and write in his native tongue. He would have kept abreast of current affairs by reading one of the numerous Welsh language newspapers then available. These tended to be politically radical, attacking English landlords and the Anglican Church which many Welsh people believed treated them unfairly.

The Welsh also bought large numbers of books. In just one year more than 50,000 Welsh Bibles were sold – a figure far in excess of any other country of comparable size. One of them found its way into the possession of the aspirant Evan Jacob and was read from frequently by his precocious daughter.

However, despite their efforts to educate and improve themselves, life for men like Evan Jacob was notoriously difficult, and they had to work hard to avoid slipping into the depths of poverty which surrounded them. At the time two shillings (ie 24 pence – equivalent in value to about £4.50 in today's money) a day would have been a good wage for a Welsh farm labourer.

Weavers and stocking knitters rarely earned more than five shilling in a week (about £10.50 today). Poor Welsh women walked up to twenty miles a day in order to gather the wool they depended upon, plucking up to 4lb a time from the gorse and bracken on the stony uplands. They could fetch a shilling for a pair of stockings it had taken them a further day to knit: a shilling that could be exchanged for not much more than a small piece of mutton. A few miles to the east, over the border, the average weekly wage was 16 shillings (worth about £35 in today's money). Small wonder that so many Welshmen put shoulder to scythe and walked to England at hay-cutting time, or dreamt of emigration to America.

Evan was respected in his community and we may

be sure that Sarah and her mother and her brothers and sisters looked up to him. But to the English authorities, he was just another ignorant, albeit crafty peasant, a man of few morals, uncivilised, backward and unclean. Government reports on Wales in the 19th century repeatedly accused the Welsh of theft, lying, cheating, drunkenness, backwardness, dirtiness and stupidity.

<hr/>

Front page, Carmarthen Weekly Reporter
Saturday 3rd April 1869
A VISIT TO SEE THE WONDERFUL
LITTLE GIRL IN CARMARTHENSHIRE
Tuesday in a 2nd class railway carriage on the Carmarthen and Cardigan Railway en route to Pencader. I reached the tolerable-sized farm at Lletherneuadd after a walk of more than two miles further. It is a low farm house at the foot of a hill, surrounded by pretty mountainous scenery close by a small village of not more than twelve houses. It consists of little more than a hovel and living-room-cum-parlour-cum-sitting-cum-bedroom where the family sleep. The barn adjoining it is of good size and well-appointed.

The little girl was lying on a low bedstead, the bedclothes being exceedingly clean. The counterpane was covered in books and pamphlets. She is very pretty, dressed with an artificial flower wreath about the head and a black shawl. She reads well in a strong voice in both Welsh and English. She read to me some poetry of her own composition.

The family are respectable farmers and in comfortable circumstances. No explanation can be offered as to the manner in which the little girl maintains life and growth. This report is made to satisfy the curiosity of the many unable to see for themselves the Welsh Fasting Girl, and to arouse the interest of those of the medical profession who may wish to pursue their own investigation into the matter...

The broad-gauge railway was first brought to Carmarthenshire in 1860, but it took another thirty-five years to reach Newcastle Emlyn – a distance of just fifteen miles. It was almost as though the effort of cutting through the mountains and the task of taming Wales had exhausted everyone. The track reached Pencader in 1864, when Sarah Jacob turned seven, heralding a time of welcome and necessary progress, though it also signalled the decline and dissolution of something uniquely Welsh.

English began to be heard on the streets of Pencader as the little town filled with the men brought over from Ireland and England to build the railway. Coming into contact with outsiders, in most cases for the first time, the local young men began to copy the railway workers, drinking and gambling. They even began to express their disappointment with the life they had previously taken for granted. Young Welsh women, exposed to English fashions for the first time, left off their quaint national costumes, the tall black hats and checked skirts, and began to imitate the manners and appearance of the strangers.

It was only a matter of time before many young people would leave the district forever, climbing aboard trains bound for Birmingham, Liverpool and, of course, London. From the 1870s onwards, in the midst of the worst decline in agriculture for more than fifty years, vast numbers of rural Welshmen and women went 'down south' in search of better prospects in the coalfields and steelworks.

So by the time Sarah Jacob reached the height of her celebrity in 1869, the 'wild Welsh' were being

THE ILLUSTRATED
POLICE  NEWS
LAW COURTS AND WEEKLY RECORD.

FRIDAY, DECEMBER 24, 1869.

Price One Pen

THE FASTING WELSH GIRL CASE. VIEW OF THE FARM HOUSE

dragged into the modern era. The many people who came to visit the Welsh Fasting Girl and her strange land were, in fact, being treated to a glimpse of an already vanishing world.

It would have taken the visitors all day, travelling at the top speed of sixty miles per hour, to reach Wales from London. Yet all through the wet spring and the wintry summer of 1869 – with its unseasonally chill north-east wind – the pilgrims continued to arrive at Pencader Junction.

There they were greeted by boys in large caps decorated with strips of paper bearing the legend: 'TO THE FASTING GIRL'. Local men wel-comed each train, parading the platform with placards advertising 'THE SHORTEST WAY TO LLETHERNEUADD-UCHAF' and offering the use of their hay-carts and ponies to those prepared to pay for the journey. Many a village child (like the mother-in-law of Mrs Waters who runs the Old Shop in Llanfihangel-ar-arth today) earned a welcome sixpence by showing ladies and gentlemen the way to Lletherneuadd. And the sixpenny bits would have been plentiful. For as soon as the Reverend Jones's letter was published in February 1869 the strangers began appearing at the farmstead, six or seven at a time, in a steady stream throughout the day.

It would have been a stiff walk from the station to Lletherneuadd. On a pleasant day, the surrounding countryside – with its neat, lush fields, gentle rolling hills and clusters of snowy-white cottages – could be very picturesque; but the Welsh weather always harbours unwelcome surprises. The sky will all of a sudden turn a sombre dark-blue, as thick grey clouds gather overhead and within moments rain will pour down upon the suddenly desolate landscape.

The lane to Llanfihangel-ar-arth was narrow and lined with thick hazel bushes, which overhung the path. It was impossible to avoid brushing against them and if that encounter didn't leave one sodden and shivering, then the chilly south-west wind, sweeping across the moors with its charge of cold mountain spray, would.

What is more, the appalling state of the Welsh roads was well known. After a heavy rainfall – and 1869 was a catastrophically wet year – the way would become criss-crossed by deep, muddy ruts and great pools of water that often reached up to the knees of a horse. Only a few intrepid souls ventured out on these roads in bad weather – even in a cart. Invariably such a journey resulted in the traveller being tipped out into the mud, when their cartwheel hit one of the piles of abandoned stones littering the road surface.

When they finally reached the humble cottage, visitors would be invited to sit and warm themselves in the kitchen before being admitted into the tiny, dark back parlour, where the Welsh Fasting Girl reclined. There she lay – her eyes glittering in the gloom – illuminated by just two candles fixed either side at the foot of her bed. She was like a bride, they said, festooned in ribbons and bows, a large crucifix resting on her bosom. Her little gloved hand strained to turn the pages of the book open in front of her, propped up on two others.

If they were specially honoured, a visitor might be permitted to clasp her tiny hand and feel the fluttering pulse while she read to them in her distinctive, clear voice from her Welsh Bible or recited one of her own religious poems. A passing dog might oblige by barking, so that Sarah could demonstrate one of her famous 'fits', in the course of which she would lie back, her eyelids flickering, breathing heavily. After a few moments, she would emit a great sigh and stretch the muscles of her face as if waking from sleep. The visitors, satisfied, would then place a few coins on the child's breast before starting on the journey back to Pencader Station and the modern world.

THE ILLUSTRATED
POLICE  NEWS
LAW COURTS AND WEEKLY RECORD
SATURDAY JANUARY 1, 1870

SARAH JACOBS IN HER BED ROOM

❧

Sarah Jacob was not the first fasting girl – there had been many before. Nor was she the last. In fact, in the spring of 1869, as her fame was spreading – written about each day in the newspapers avidly read by thousands all over the country, visited by scores of eager pilgrims – Sarah already had a rival. There was a young girl in Ulverston who 'it is said, has... been twenty-five weeks without any food passing her lips and sixteen without having her lips moistened.'

At the end of May, the *Illustrated London News* was pleased to report that this pretender had begun to eat and walk again and Sarah's singular claim to fame was thus restored. At the height of the media frenzy following Sarah's death, an anguished father was moved to write to the *Standard* with the tale of his own daughter who had eaten only 'very, very little in many months', in spite of a corrective spell in St Thomas's Hospital. And the year after Sarah's case had been resolved, Ann Riding of Preston was admitted to an infirmary at the mayor's request, in order that she be induced to eat.

In the remaining decades of the nineteenth century,

teenage fasting girls the length and breadth of the British Isles continued to attract media interest: Ellen Sudworth of Lancashire who ate nothing solid for four years; Martha White 'the Market Harborough Fasting Girl'; Glasgow's Christina Marshall; Maggie Sutherland on Orkney. There was even another 'Welsh Fasting Girl'.

However, not one of them was able to capture the public imagination in the way that Sarah Jacob did. Her life coincided with great changes in the world: blind faith was giving way to empiricism, the evidence revealed by the scalpel and the microscope. In the decade after Sarah's death, the doctors put a name to the mysterious ailment which apparently afflicted her – *anorexia nervosa* – and suddenly the days of the miraculous fasting girls were officially over. There was no mystery, there were no young women able to live on the vital magnetism imbibed from surrounding organisms, on air, on the power of their own faith. There was just 'hysteria'. The days of superstition were numbered with the passing of the Welsh Fasting Girl of Lletherneuadd.

The earlier case of Ann Moore, the notorious 'Fasting Woman of Tutbury', had spelled the beginning of the end. Her cautionary tale was regularly invoked in reference to Sarah Jacob, especially in the medical and scientific journals. Ann Moore was an impoverished mother of two illegitimate children when she stopped eating in 1807. She claimed that she had been suddenly overcome with a physical revulsion towards all food after washing the sheets of her employer (the father of her two children) – a man with a particularly disgusting ulcerous skin complaint.

The longer she starved herself the more religious Ann Moore became, and before long she had acquired a reputation as a powerful mystic. As her fame grew, however, she began to attract the attention of scientists and religious leaders. Anxious lest the emaciated woman with her popular religious and moral pronouncements made a mockery of their learning and authority, they decided to put a watch on her.

It took just one week for the truth about Ann Moore to reveal itself. Denied access to the means by which she habitually obtained nourishment – a handkerchief seeped in vinegar and water, morsels of food passed in the act of kissing her daughter, a night-dress sleeve dipped in starch – she was quickly brought to death's door and there confessed her crime. The Fasting Woman of Tutbury was held up as an example of female deceit for many years to come.

In Wales, women had long made fasting something of a speciality. In the forgotten, backward land just across the Severn, where it was easy to find grown men who believed in fairies, people were still prepared to accept that women who starved themselves were endowed with an excess of wisdom and fulgent spirituality. There had been at least two celebrated Welsh fasting women who, in the century before Sarah Jacob embarked on her career as anorexic *mirabilis*, secured a place for themselves in local mythology and the world beyond. Their ears had rung with the bardic verses sung in their praise; they had been the subject of charming illustrations by acclaimed artists; their plain, humble dwellings had been enlivened by handsome London bucks and fine ladies in coloured silks and richly-woven shawls.

Twenty-seven-year-old Mary Thomas had stopped eating following a short illness and took no food whatsoever for two years – vomiting blood whenever she tried. She was deathly pale and extremely thin, but nonetheless lived to the ripe old age of eighty-four, subsisting on no more than a few crumbs of bread, drops of water and the occasional glass of wine.

Her near neighbour, Gaunor Hughes, as celebrated as Sarah Jacob in her time, was extremely beautiful, even though she was positively skeletal, her bones clearly visible through her paper-thin skin. For eight years in the last quarter of the eighteenth century, she had lain in a straw bed over the byre of her family home, unable to bear the sight or smell of food. She lived on one spoonful of water a day and was visited with vivid, symbol-rich hallucinations. Many came to hear her describe and interpret them. She lives on as part of the folklore of Llandderfel, where the well she drank from still bears her name.

Sarah Jacob would have heard tell of these women and others like them. She may even have aspired to share their celebrity. In the village of Cynwil Elfed, six miles across the mountains from Llanfihangel-ar-arth, folk were still recounting an even stranger case in the early years of the twentieth century. A young servant girl was sent to call in the cows one evening, and inadvertently stepped into a fairy ring. She subsequently lived for a long time without food and without ever feeling hungry.

⁂

When land is gone and money spent,
Then learning is most excellent…

Old Welsh Proverb

Sarah, like the rest of her family, had survived the scarlet fever, in February 1866, apparently unscathed. Hannah and Evan, with the stoicism typical of hardy peasants with little spare money, had self-diagnosed and didn't think it worth the trouble and expense of calling in Dr Harries Davies. Within a couple of weeks, Sarah was back at the village church school. She was a firm favourite of its founder, the Reverend Evan Jones, who was impressed by her 'above ordinary intelligence' and considered her to be 'a precocious child', but ladylike and well-behaved, 'never particularly seeking the society or play of the other sex...'

For the next year or so, things seem to have progressed favourably in Sarah's life. She carried on with her studies, even though most little girls from her station in life would have received no education at all – only forty per cent of the total female population in the 1860s were considered worth teaching. Even after the 1870 Elementary Education Act made attendance at school compulsory, it was a right extended only to children under ten. Youngsters like Sarah were expected to contribute to the family income; the long school summer holiday was incepted in order that children could help bring in the summer harvests, and as late as 1891 ten-year-olds could still be found working in coalmines.

Evan and Hannah evidently had aspirations for their children, but they were also pragmatic people. Sarah, at nine years old, would have been required to take her turn in helping her mother in the home. Like most little girls, she would be kept from school on occasion to help on washing day and would soon develop the strong arm muscles required for wringing out linen and hand-churning butter. Her big sisters Mary and Esther would be looking forward to the day when they would marry and set up homes of their own, leaving Sarah behind to help her mother until it was her turn to escape from her father's home into a domestic servitude of her own devising.

Who had ever heard of a Welsh peasant's daughter growing up to be a famous poetess, or a preacher? Apart from the fasting girls, Sarah could draw inspiration from the sixteen-year-old weaver's daughter, Mary Jones, who in 1800 had walked fifty miles, barefoot, across the Gwynedd mountains in search of her own Welsh language Bible. Her story was still being held up as an example to little girls at Chapel Sunday schools in my own childhood.

Sarah would probably also have heard of Anne Griffiths, from Llanfyllin in Powys, who ran an isolated smallholding single-handed, the monotony and effort of her days relieved by the religious poems which 'came to her' as she worked in the fields. She never wrote them down, but she did teach them to her illiterate companion, Ruth Evans, who, when Anne died in childbirth, in 1805, aged just thirty, dictated them to a scribe so that they would not be forgotten. At nine years old, Sarah's life was already stretching out in front of her and the bright and beautiful child faced a stark choice – to find fulfilment in drudgery, or piety. As it was, fate interceded in a surprising way.

On the morning of 15th February 1867 Sarah awoke with a sharp pain in her stomach. She went to school as usual, but when she came home that afternoon she informed her mother that she had spat up some blood. It was a Monday – washing day – and Hannah had spent hours elbow-deep in caustic soda crystals, her face red and dripping from the steam of the copper and the effort of scrubbing and heaving dead weights of wet linen.

She reacted to her daughter's news with the brusqueness of any overworked mother of six, and diagnosed a cold. But the child's pains worsened and two days later Hannah was sufficiently concerned to keep Sarah from school. The girl never went to school again. Hannah put her to bed in the parlour away from the other children, and there she remained until her death nearly three years later.

After a couple more days in which Sarah cried piteously, frequently complaining of internal pains, Hannah summoned the family doctor, Henry Harries Davies, MRCS, from Llandyssul. Dr Davies was in his early thirties, relatively young and inexperienced. He was unsure how to treat Sarah, but gave her some medicine, which eased the tummy pains, and diagnosed some sort of chest infection.

Over the course of the next month, however, Sarah's condition worsened into something beyond the young doctor's experience and skill. Although Evan Jacob alleged that the doctor had merely treated Sarah for worms, Dr Davies would later claim that he had diagnosed 'catalepsy' and had recommended a diet of *sopa* (buttermilk and oatmeal).

In the nineteenth century 'catalepsy' was a somewhat fashionable catch-all description for a host of illnesses, which were accompanied by seizures, paralysis and behavioural disturbances. It was a diagnosis given almost exclusively to teenage girls, and was often associated with mental or physical disturbance at the onset of menstruation.

Sarah's parents and Dr Davies were at least agreed on one thing: she had been unconscious for the six weeks the doctor had been in attendance – in some sort of fit, rigid on the left side and becoming increasingly skeletal. The Jacobs, for their part, stuck to Dr Davies's remedy for six long weeks, while Sarah lay on her back.

Not surprisingly, when there was no improvement, they sought a second opinion. Dr Harries Davies had, in any case, pronounced himself totally baffled by the case and in April 1867 he gave up treating Sarah altogether, 'knowing', as he later informed the newspapers, that 'medical aid was of no avail'.

After one dreadful night when her parents fully expected Sarah to die, Davies proclaimed that Sarah was in the hands of '*y doctor mawr*' (the great doctor, i.e. God) and withdrew from the case, saying 'it was of no use, only to spend money'.

The second doctor the Jacobs consulted, Dr Hopkins, attended Sarah just once at the beginning of April 1867. He diagnosed inflammation of the brain – incurable, alas – and regretted that he had not been consulted some nine days earlier when he might have been able to save the poor girl. He prescribed two pills, but the comatose child was unable to swallow anything.

After this, with Sarah apparently close to death, Dr Harries Davies was persuaded to return to Lletherneuadd. She had not eaten anything for a month and had only had her lips moistened with small quantities of water and table beer. However, after two days Sarah suddenly regained consciousness and sat up in bed asking for some milk. Dr Harries Davies administered an enema (a practice which involved inserting a tube into the back passage, and then pumping warm soapy water into the bowels to 'clean' them out). The little girl then passed some urine and after two weeks Harries Davies signed off the case, leaving detailed instructions regarding the child's diet.

What ailed Sarah continues to perplex. The correct diagnosis of her illness was probably far beyond the medical knowledge of the time. In the 1860s, science and medicine were still not considered entirely serious and suitable subjects for gentlemen to study at public schools and universities. The licensing of doctors was less than a decade old and the infectious nature of a whole range of diseases, including tuberculosis, had yet to be recognised. In the pages of some journals, serious consideration was given to the idea of treating cancer with lightening bolts.

The medical historian, Dr John Cule, in his authoritative 1967 examination of the case, *Wreath on the Crown*, concluded that Sarah was possibly suffering from viral encephalitis. This illness – inflammation of the brain caused by a viral infection – often starts with gastrointestinal disturbance and its symptoms include fever, convulsions, partial paralysis and vomiting. It has a high-mortality rate, with death resulting from pressure on the brain and its impact on the central nervous system. Survivors are often left with some vestigial brain damage, and Sarah's behaviour certainly became increasingly disturbed after the initial phase of the illness.

True, the autopsy found no trace of trauma or injury on the surface of the brain, but that is not entirely surprising: Sarah may well have been suffering from a virus not detectable in the 1860s. At the time, however, the absence of any physical signs pointed, irrefutably, to some form of mental illness. In keeping with the thinking of the time, Sarah Jacob was obviously suffering from 'hysteria'.

Nobody around her seems to have considered that Sarah's illness may have been the result of a profound emotional trauma – perhaps one suffered at school or on the long walk to and from school, such as a sexual attack. It would not have taken much to cause intense emotional disturbance to a deeply religious young girl from a very sheltered background. Certainly if something of this type did occur, Sarah doesn't appear to have ever told anyone.

Whether the reason lay in psychological and/or physical causes, what is known is that, in the second phase of her illness, she stopped eating, and eating disorders are nowadays often diagnosed as the symptom of severe neurosis deriving from an unconscious refusal to accept physically and sexually mature. Between mid-April and the end of August, Sarah managed no more than six cupfuls of rice and milk. She grew pitifully thin and her lovely thick hair fell out. She was evidently gravely ill and required constant nursing. Two or three times a day her parents attempted to feed her as per the doctor's instructions, but the little girl was unable to swallow and vomited up everything she was given – often with blood. She suffered violent fits and was unable to leave her bed at all. Her left leg was in a state of constant rigidity.

Her parents did all they could to keep their ailing child comfortable. As the autumn drew on and the nights grew colder in the freezing back parlour, Sarah's beloved little sister Margaret was encouraged to sleep with her. It seemed to help.

Sometime in February 1867, around about the time Sarah had first become ill, Hannah had fallen pregnant with her seventh child. Now, as her time approached, it was the haymaking period when Hannah was required to cook for and generally look after the men hired to help with the pitching and baling. At one of the busiest times of the farming year, with a baby on the way, both parents had to find additional time and energy to nurse an invalid child. Evan, mindful of the pressures on his wife, started to make Sarah's bed for her every other day, laying her on his and Hannah's bed while he shook the thin mattress and changed the frequently wet sheets. Sarah began to make a fuss if anyone other than her 'dadda' tried to make the bed and Evan was proud that nobody, not even Hannah 'could make it so well or so smooth'. He continued to make Sarah's bed for her until she died.

All this attention notwithstanding, as the months wore on Sarah became more and more difficult to deal with. The merest suggestion that she might eat something, the very sight of food, was enough to throw her into convulsions. Back in August she had managed to eat a small apple dumpling each day, but by October this had been reduced to 'a little apple, about the size of a pill, in a teaspoon', taken once in the morning and once in the evening. Her parents were frantic with worry and, unaided by the doctor who had not been near them since the spring, they began to formulate their own opinion about their little girl's condition.

At about this time, Evan noticed that Sarah was no longer thin although she still 'looked very bad in the face', and it occurred to him and Hannah that Sarah was somehow managing to thrive on very little food. They wondered if the attempts made to feed her – rather than the meagreness of the diet – were some-how exacerbating her condition. Perhaps if they tried just tending to her needs for comfort and affection and stopped making the offers of food that so obviously distressed her... They followed their instincts for a few days and saw an immediate improvement in Sarah's condition. The hysterical outbursts and bloody vomit, which had, up until then, characterised her illness, ended. The distressing fits evolved into something gen-tler and more like a temporary loss of consciousness than a convulsion.

On 10th October 1867, with the full agreement of both her parents, Sarah Jacob stopped taking food altogether. Evan and Hannah, who was now in the final stages of her pregnancy, made a *llw* (word of honour). With great solemnity over the family Bible, they swore that they would never again offer Sarah any more food unless she asked for some. Over the ensuing weeks, neighbours began to pay visits to Hannah and her daughter as the rumour spread across the valley that something wondrous and strange was happening at the Jacob's farm. Hannah, desperately sorry for her poor bedridden little girl who had no more pleasure in life, began to decorate Sarah in ribbons and bows. And the legend of the Welsh Fasting Girl was born.

...The house is in a picturesque, warm valley. It is a rather small old farmhouse. The parents and family are plainly clad, the elder girls were milking the cows and the younger children were in the kitchen. Fine, healthy-looking boys and girls; well-behaved and quiet...

(letter to the Carmarthen Weekly Reporter
Saturday 22nd May 1869)

Sarah's mother was born Hannah Williams in 1830, and had lived in Llanfihangel-ar-arth her entire life. Her two sisters lived near by and so did her parents.

Her younger sister Martha was married to a tailor, John Daniel, who kept a well-appointed drapery store in Pencader that Sarah, in happier times, had liked to visit.

Hannah was tiny – just over five foot one. She appears distracted and bewildered in the only photograph of her, taken shortly after Sarah's death, squinting against the light. From under her bonnet it is just possible to make out her very Welsh features – high, pointed, but not sharp, cheekbones, a small mouth and hooded eyes. She is wearing a gown with cape-shoulders, buttoned up to the chin, and her dark hair is decorated either side with some floral decoration, not unlike that with which she used to adorn Sarah's hair.

By the end of 1867 Evan and Hannah had seven children: Sarah, then aged ten, eighteen-year-old Mary, Esther (fourteen), Evan Saunders (nine), Samuel (six), Margaret (five) and the baby David, born in November. By all accounts, the children were handsome, healthy, well behaved and well looked after. Hannah's brother-in-law testified that she and Evan 'were good and kind to their children' and, unusually for the time, Hannah doesn't appear to have lost any children in infancy by this stage. The family were evidently good managers and Hannah an efficient and capable mother.

The Jacobs' eldest daughter, Mary, is entered on the baptismal register of the parish church as Mary Williams – Hannah's maiden name – which may mean that she was born before Hannah and Evan were married. Many Welsh couples practised what was called 'caru-ar-y-gwely' ('courting in bed', or 'bundling'), something which only added to their reputation for immoral, pagan behaviour in the eyes of those English authorities who had denounced the custom as 'the great sin of Wales'.

All nine of the Jacobs lived in just a few small rooms at Lletherneuadd. The kitchen, the family's main living area, was small by modern standards – about twelve foot by nine – with doors leading off it to the other rooms. These cottage kitchens were normally kept very cosy, but were very dark with just one small window and the fire continually smoking in an open hearth in the corner.

The hearth at Lletherneuadd was not much more than a few coals laid on the mud floor, leading up to a hole in the roof through which the sky could be glimpsed, but as in ancient Celtic times, it was the centre of the home. Well into the twentieth century there were hearth fires in Welsh homes that had never been allowed to go out. Each night when the fire was dismantled, an ember would be picked out and carefully covered with ashes so that it could provide the spark for the kindling laid the following morning. Hannah would have been careful to maintain her hearth fire in this time-honoured way, but she kept the rest of the house – especially the dairy – very cold. The back bedroom, or parlour, where Evan and Hannah slept and where Sarah was put after she became ill, had not been heated for at least two years by the time she died in there.

Pride of place in the kitchen went to the dresser, on which Hannah would have arranged all her best china. This and the simple rug lying on the mud floor would have afforded some of the only colour in the otherwise gloomy house. There was a comfortable settle and a chair by the fire for Evan to sit in of an evening while he smoked his pipe and read his newspaper. Under the window by the front door was a large round table, around which every night the family would gather to eat and take turns to read from the Welsh Bible before going to bed.

Between the byre and the kitchen lay the tiny room where all the Jacob children slept. There was also a loft in the eaves, reached by a ladder from the kitchen, where the Jacobs' servant would have lodged under the leaky thatch and above the byre, with the smells and the rats that go along with cattle and straw. The tiny narrow window of the loft can still be seen on the east end wall of the house (now used as a barn), just above the place where Sarah herself slept in relative comfort and privacy until she died. In 1861 the live-in servant was a woman by the name of Jane Davies, no doubt employed to help Hannah with the children (three of them under five). By 1869 the servant was a man, who helped Evan with his growing farm. This farm-servant, overworked and exhausted most of the time, is something of a shadowy figure, surprisingly never questioned by anyone about the events that happened in the farmstead and who took whatever he knew with him to the grave.

The cottage had a mud floor, so it would have been damp and claggy for most of the year, and keeping it and its inhabitants clean would have been a full-time job for Hannah. Evan had a hard, tough life, but he could at least escape into the active role of a respected citizen, attending chapel meetings and the markets and fairs in Pencader and beyond. His wife and daughters, however, led lives of relentless labour, with few opportunities to relax. Housework had to be fitted in around the work of the farm, and the volume and difficulty of it depended upon the seasons; but all year round it would have been arduous and monotonous – and always to be completed before the Sabbath. The weeks would have worn on ineluctably: washing day on Mondays, baking day on Wednesdays, churning day on Fridays. In between there were the demands of three young children, a baby to be nursed and Sarah – to all intents completely bedridden.

All of Monday was given over to the laundry. Washing the linen and clothing for nine people, by hand, with abrasive washing soda, was backbreaking, spirit-crushing work. There was no running water, so pails had to be fetched, in all weather, from either the river or the well and boiled over the fire in heavy copper cauldrons. Some farmsteads gathered rainwater in barrels as it dripped from the eaves, but Lletherneuadd was thatched, so only minimal amounts of the plentiful Welsh rainfall could have been accumulated in this way. Hannah kept two large linen-presses in the parlour, but in fine weather she would have dried her washing first by lying it on the ground outside – many housewives believed that the grass made the linen whiter.

On rainy days and in the colder months she would hang it out on a line over the kitchen fire, where it would quickly become sooty and grimy – if it didn't go mouldy first. The washing might be left hanging there for days, but it had to be taken down before baking day or the smell of the baking would be upon it. Once a fortnight the corduroy trousers worn by the men had to be scrubbed rigorously until all the mud and muck had been removed.

Welsh countrywomen took great pride in the spotless appearance of their man's work trousers. In spite of the extra work entailed, Sarah had fresh sheets two or three times each week and her visitors constantly remarked upon her immaculate bed linen. Hannah would have acknowledged all such praise in that very Welsh way – a curt nod of the head belying the deep sense of pride and satisfaction she would have felt. Her intense desire to prove that she and her family were as good as anyone was shared by her daughter, who was always most anxious to look 'smart' before receiving her visitors, insisting on a clean flannel nightdress every day.

Although they were not financially dependent upon knitting, as many of their neighbours would have been, Hannah and her daughters stitched and knitted

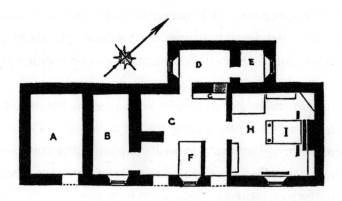

Ground plan of the Jacobs' farmhouse

A, Cow-house; B, Servant's bedroom; C, Kitchen;
D, Back-kitchen; E, Dairy; F, Table; G, Dresser; H, Parent's and
Sarah Jacob's Bedroom; I, The Fasting Girl's bedstead

most of the clothes worn by the family. Welsh women were prodigious knitters, and performed the task unthinkingly with impressive rapidity. My grandmother's grand-mother – a Cardi farmer's daughter, born in 1842 – taught her daughters and granddaughters to knit quickly and skilfully. She also imparted in them a keen pride in keeping their homes spotless, their linens snowy-white. English people, they were told, thought the Welsh were dirty. The Welsh had to prove that they were not. My Nan had an aunt who still washed all her linen by hand when she was well into her late eighties.

Auntie's weekly wash consisted of a dozen table-clothes, two dozen teacloths, the sheets and pillowcases from four beds – all washed without the aid of modern technology.

Hannah and her daughters were also responsible for preparing the food, not just for the family, but also for the men employed to help with the haymaking and baling. The task of keeping such a large number of people clothed, clean and fed would have taken up almost every moment of Hannah's day.

Like their neighbours, the Jacobs relied upon a frugal and unchanging diet of home-baked bread, buttermilk, watery cheese, mashed potato and oats. The cawl was generally started at nine in the morning and kept on the go until mid-day. A little bit of bacon or mutton, if either were available, would be added first, followed by the vegetables, then the oatmeal and finally the leeks. Some women baked only once a fortnight, but most baked once a week – usually on a Wednesday – preparing seven flat loaves and piles of Welsh cakes on a bakestone over the open fire. Hannah would have instructed her girls in the best way to pot fish and, when available, preserve pork and salt beef.

Though basic, the staple diet of the Welsh was very healthy. The ready supply of milk helped to maintain their reputation as a 'muscular and robust race, capable of undergoing great labour', according to the national food inquiry of 1863. Much of the milk yield from Lletherneuadd's herd would have been taken to the railway station at Pencader and put on the milk train, bound for London – until well into the twentieth century, most of London's milk came from Wales – but it also went to feed the family.

The important task of milking took place once in the early morning and once in the late afternoon and was carried out by the two older daughters, Mary and Esther. The cattle were milked out in the field, where the girls sat on low stools, stooped over the waiting pail, their heads pressed into the warm underside of the beast. In the freezing winter months and into the early spring, the cows were brought out of the byre and milked in the yard. It was not uncommon in rural Wales for close attachments to form between families and their milch cows.

Cattle were vital for survival, and the Welsh word '*da*' – goodness – was traditionally synonymous with livestock, the source of livelihood for many families down the ages. Even today Welsh farms are often evaluated in terms of the number of cows they can sustain.

The dairy at Lletherneuadd was a later addition to the building, abutting the back wall of the main part of the house. It was reached via the kitchen, but in contrast to the muddy, smoky gloom of the main room, was scrupulously clean and very cold. In here, Hannah and her daughters made butter, buttermilk and cheese. Butter was often used as a form of currency in West Wales and paid as 'wages' for help in bringing in the harvest or for the services of a boar or bull. Its manufacture was an essential part of the weekly routine. A small oversight or neglect of duty at any stage would have resulted in a wasted batch, ruinous for the family.

Every Tuesday a little milk was placed in the setting-dish and left overnight in order to separate the cream. This would then be placed in a stone vessel covered with a piece of muslin and left to ripen for two days. At least an hour of every Friday was given over to turning the churn until the arms ached and the butter was gradually formed from the cream, thickening as it slapped around the walls of the barrel. Great care had to be taken not to over-churn the butter in warm weather, and in cold weather it might be necessary to add a drop of warm milk to help the stubborn butter come. In the winter months, when the cattle lived on turnips, the butter would be almost colourless, but in the summer months, when the grazing was good, it would have the rich sheen of buttercups. Once formed, the butter was pounded with pats until all the whey was squeezed out of it, going to make the buttermilk – as important in the old Welsh diet as potatoes were to the Irish.

Cheesemaking required even more time and care. Large copper vats had to be heated to just the right temperature and stirred constantly before the rennet could be added. Then followed the lengthy, painstaking process of scalding and separating the junket. Once ready, the cheese was pressed into moulds and wrapped in muslin. It was left on a cold shelf and turned every day for a fortnight in the winter, twice a day in summer, and then every other day until it was ripe.

The presence of a dairy in the homestead meant that there would be no difficulty for any member of the Jacob family seeking access to a steady, if meagre, supply of food. In the dairy, milk sat in churns, cream rested in setting dishes, crumbs of cheese nestled the big round. In the kitchen a pile of loaves resided in the crock and a seemingly bottomless pot of cawl was suspended in the hearth.

The family and the hired hands would have simply helped themselves whenever they could take a break from their work. Nothing was precisely measured, so small amounts taken regularly would hardly have been missed at all. While everyone was out in the farmyard and the fields, a clever girl might easily entice a little brother or sister to fetch themselves a bowl of bread and milk or 'a little bit of fishy', and persuade or trick them into letting her partake of it.

At night, her exhausted parents, the curtains drawn close around their bed, privacy being especially desirous with an impressionable girl sharing their room, could be relied upon not to stir as she crept out of bed. Once in the dairy, the fairies would skitter into the dark corners, slyly peeping out from behind the churns as she filled up her secret bottle with a ladle or two of buttermilk.

❧

> Q: Who made you?
> A: God made me.
>> *1st Question of the Children's*
>> *Catechism of the Anglican Church*

Around the time her baby brother was born in November 1867, Sarah started to voice fears for her mortal soul. Since her parents had stopped forcing her to eat, she appeared to be much healthier, and was enjoying an unprecedented amount of their attention. Was something now weighing on her conscience? Or had the birth of a little brother – in the same room in which Sarah herself was lying – disturbed the sensitive child?

The family attended Chapel rather than Church, but it was her old friend, the Anglican vicar Reverend Jones, who Sarah asked to come and baptise her. He probably administered the Sacrament to Sarah at the beginning of November. It is perhaps surprising that a family who were, like the majority of Welsh, strict Nonconformists and therefore opposed to the Anglican Church's enforced domination of Wales, should permit their child to be received into that Church.

Every Sunday the Jacobs walked for an hour to their Chapel, where they would have lent their voices to the charismatic 'praising', and given their assent to the explicitly anti-English feelings often expressed in the sermons. However, even in rural Carmarthenshire, where less than twenty-five per cent of the population were Church of England, most people accepted that a Welshman seeking a successful career in trade or one of the professions needed to be in possession of an Anglican baptism and some grasp of the English language. The Jacobs, quite simply, wanted the best for their children.

The relationship with Evan Jones, however, went far beyond mere convenience. The staid vicar and the rugged farmer clearly liked each other a great deal, and, in spite of their religious differences, enjoyed a rapport and mutual respect which remained even after Sarah was no longer there to provide a common focus and bond.

Whenever called upon to do so, Reverend Jones always presented Evan and Hannah in a good light, depicting them as affectionate parents, a couple who seemed to 'pull well together'.

Perhaps we can read into all of this solicitousness the workings of a guilty conscience on the vicar's part; perhaps he felt that he was, in some way, responsible for Sarah's fate. Certainly, many others did, but the Jacobs were not among them. They were remarkably trusting people, and do not appear to have ever borne any ill-will towards him. They always reciprocated his friendship.

In November 1867, when he was summoned to Sarah Jacob's bedside for the first time, Reverend Jones was in the prime of life, in his late thirties, with a distinguished career as Rector of Newport still ahead of him. He was happily married with one baby daughter and another on the way and enjoying the comfortable living at Llanfihangel-ar-arth – worth a solid £179 per year and with a sixty-four acre farm attached to it. He was a local boy made good.

A graduate of St David's, Lampeter, the nearby centre of theology training for those bright young men who could not afford to go to Oxford or Cambridge, he had lived among his parishioners for most of his life and was familiar with their ways and the occasionally surprising pattern of their faith. A hardworking and committed parish priest, he strove to reconcile the opposing forces of the Welsh Chapel and the Anglican Church. No doubt many would tell him he was fighting a losing battle, but he was resourceful and dedicated and rarely discouraged.

He well knew that most of his parishioners preferred to walk several miles across hills in all weather to reach the chapel of their choice, rather than attend his sermons; but, being a native son, Reverend Jones also understood that the church represented a valued continuum with the past (for one thing, the ancestors of almost all local people were buried there) and he knew how to turn that to good account. Reverend Jones read his sermons in Welsh and almost as soon as he arrived in the village devoted his energies to establishing a school. In all probability, Sarah was among the seventy children who sang a specially composed song to the tune of 'Home Sweet Home', when the foundations were laid for the new purpose-built school that he opened in 1864.

She soon became the Reverend Jones's favourite pupil. When she became ill and could no longer attend school, he visited her every week and remained her most loyal friend until she died, even though in doing so he exposed himself to a barrage of ridicule. He seems never to have tired of her company, sitting for long periods at her bedside. The pair enjoyed intense religious discussions, in which Sarah astonished the vicar with her prodigious ability to quote chapter and verse from the Bible.

Given all this, it is perhaps a little curious that in his memoirs Reverend Jones makes only a passing reference to his little friend. Perhaps he wanted to distance himself from the notoriety surrounding the affair; or sought to protect himself and Sarah's family from the idle curiosity of others or the tangle of any more misunderstanding. Maybe he simply felt that he had nothing more to say about the strange, gifted little girl whose sad end he had witnessed and, some would say, unwittingly wrought. Who can tell?

Certainly, at the start of the mysterious goings-on at Lletherneuadd, the Reverend had been somewhat sceptical, and he stated as much at the inquest. When Hannah first made her claims for Sarah, saying that 'she thought it was a miracle', he had told her 'it was not a miracle'. He had noticed that the longer Sarah refused food, the more plump and healthy she became and, his suspicions aroused, had warned the Jacobs about the dangers of deception. He alleged he was exasperated by their stubborn declaration that 'no imposture would be found in their house, because there was none'. And yet it was the sensible, educated vicar and not the gullible parents who went on to write a letter to the newspapers claiming there could be 'no doubt whatever' that Sarah was a true fasting girl.

It is not known precisely when the Reverend Jones came to form his surprising conviction about the true nature of events at Lletherneuadd. What is certain is that after he had been visiting Sarah for several months, he suffered a shattering blow within his own family. In June 1868 his young wife Elizabeth died of typhoid fever, leaving him with two little daughters – one a baby of just two months old. While he was mourning his loss, precipitous events occurred in the outside world – events that threatened to engulf everything the Reverend believed in.

In November 1868 there was an election in England and Wales, an event which highlighted the hostility between the two nations. This was the first election in which many Welsh tenant farmers were able to vote, but it was not a fair contest. Most Welshmen wanted to vote Liberal but their landlords were Tories. Some men were forced to vote against their principles. Others, who refused to do what their landlords said, were evicted from their farms, and made homeless.

We can imagine the effect of these tumultuous events on an intelligent and sensitive man such as the Reverend Jones – a man who was caught between two worlds. For this conservative Anglican vicar, whose sense of wellbeing, not to say livelihood, depended upon the status quo, it now appeared as if all the certainties upon which he had built his life were being threatened. First had come the railway with its crooked values and devilish enticements; now he faced daily clamourings for the overthrow of the Anglican Church in Wales.

The period between his wife's death and the publication of his letter about Sarah Jacob in the *Welshman* would therefore have been an anxious time for the Reverend. No doubt his visits to Sarah offered some relief – an opportunity to reflect upon the possibility that miracles, in the shape of a beautiful, clever and altogether entrancing child, could happen. It takes no great leap of imagination, then, to understand how, by February 1869, he was prepared to declare in cold print his belief that this 'wonderful little girl' had 'not partaken of a single grain of food whatever in the last sixteen months'. He had witnessed at first hand the extraordinary power the little girl at Lletherneuadd had over people and what he had seen had convinced him that there were things in heaven and earth that could not be explained. How could he have predicted that his letter was to push him – and the Jacob family – headlong into catastrophe?

The vicar's letter began to take effect almost immediately – after all it was not every day that an Anglican priest acknowledged a miracle. As the first uninvited visitors started to arrive at Lletherneuadd in mid-March, vituperative opinions were exchanged in the correspondence pages of the newspapers over 'The Strange Case in Carmarthenshire'. In May the newly-launched *Western Mail* told its readers, 'We candidly confess we can scarcely write with calmness of this disgraceful case', and continued to make frequent attacks on the Jacob family and their supporters for the rest of the year.

But it was the *Lancet* that most vehemently took up the cudgel against superstition, and the Reverend Jones who was their main target. The house journal of the British Medical Association, the *Lancet* was at the forefront of the movement pressing for the increased professionalisation of medical practice and was obliged to rise to any challenge to science, progress and modernity. It therefore employed its most crushing condescension in editorial after editorial to discredit the superstition and credulity of Reverend Jones. He was roundly mocked for his ignorance of elementary biology and chemistry. 'What would the Vicar say', asked the editor at the beginning of May 1869, 'if told that his neighbour's candle had been burning for sixteen months without any diminution of its tallow?'

The Reverend must have been astonished that such a shower of scorn and abuse could be rained down upon him in response to what was – at worst – a naïve gesture. He was provoked into denouncing the whole of medical science as 'the most uncertain and immature of all sciences'. The same medical science, it ought to be said, which had failed to prevent Reverend Jones's young wife from being taken from him less than a year before.

Not put off by the insults heaped upon his fellow Welshman, Sarah's family doctor, Henry Harries Davies, joined the fray in a letter to *Seren Cymru*. In an ill-disguised attempt to build his reputation as a serious medical man at the centre of a controversial and fascinating case, he set out his early involvement, his diagnosis of catalepsy – and his unequivocal acceptance that a girl could indeed live on very little. If it was all a big con trick, as the *Lancet* and *Western Mail* hinted, then he failed to see the motive.

'All the neighbours don't for a moment doubt the veracity of the thing,' he wrote, and 'the parents are perfectly willing for persons to watch that patient.' He concluded by confessing that he was truly 'perplexed, well knowing that nothing is impossible in the sight of the Creator and Preserver of all mankind.' And so the

Fasting Girl debate gathered steam and rumbled on...
Almost without anyone noticing, the little back parlour at Lletherneuadd had become a battleground in
the war between science and faith.

❦

THE SINGULAR CASE OF FASTING
  To The Editor
  Cambria Daily Leader

Wednesday 11th March 1869
        Resolved on making an
investigation I took the rail to Pencader and reached
the farm in the company of Reverend Jones. I found
the girl, Sarah Jacob, lying on her back in bed in the
parents' bedroom... I was very much struck with the
intelligent and pleasant aspect of her countenance...
The brow is smooth and round, indicating
phrenologically large organs of form, individuality
and comparison... The head measures 20 and a half
inch circumference... The region occupied by self-
esteem and firmness is perhaps the lowest. The
organs [indicate]much mental susceptibility and
cerebral activity... she is energetic and courageous in
disposition... the region indicating cautiousness is

*large... the type of head belongs to the literary and
artistic class...*

> J. Burns, Lecturer on Phrenology,
> Physiology &c
> 1 Wellington Road, Camberwell,
> London SE

❧

Barely a month after Reverend Jones's letter had made its appearance in print, on 15th March 1869, Evan Jacob took up an invitation to meet with several gentlemen, including Dr Harries Davies, Reverend Jones and some 'respectable farmers'. The meeting took place at the National Schoolroom in Llanfihangel-ararth – the site of Sarah's former triumphs. An impromptu committee was formed, with Reverend Jones as chairman, its intention to devise the most satisfactory method of 'watching and testing the case of Sarah Jacob, the young girl who is represented as not having taken any food during the past eighteen months.'

To this end, it was decided that men, in groups of two, would be selected to watch Sarah in two shifts from eight until eight each day for the fortnight between 22nd March and 5th April. The watchers would be required to swear an oath in front of the magistrate that 'should bind them not to leave a single moment pass without one of them remaining in the presence of the girl.' They would be permitted to check the items used when Evan made Sarah's bed, but nobody seems to have insisted that the bed itself – a cupboard bed with all sorts of little nooks and crannies, shelves and so forth where food could easily have been secreted – should also be scrutinised. No doubt the suggestion that Sarah herself be checked never even occurred to the strictly moral men of the village. Her father would, in any case, not have allowed such a flagrant disregard of his little girl's modesty. Nor did anybody seek to prevent Sarah's parents and, significantly, her little sister Margaret from visiting her as often as they wanted throughout the entire period of the watch.

The committee did, however, give due consideration to the cost of the watch. From now on, all visitors to the Fasting Girl were to be asked for a contribution and any surplus monies were to be sent to the local hospital. The good Chapel-going men of the committee wound up by declaring that there was to be 'No Sunday Visiting' at Lletherneuadd.

The watchers were seven in total; two of them,

interestingly, nephews of Dr Harries Davies. He must have been worried about looking foolish, having announced in the press his belief that Sarah was miraculous. No doubt, his nephews could be relied upon to protect his interests.

In other respects, however, the doctor and Reverend Jones were keen to ensure that every effort was made to keep everything above board. Dr Harries Davies made some attempt to find qualified, independent witnesses, writing to three medical men from different parts of Wales, asking them to recommend trustworthy men from their own locality to act as watchers. Only one of the doctors bothered to reply. Mr James Rowlands of a nearby village sent along one John Jones to act as a watcher. Rowlands would also agree, later on, to be part of the medical committee established to further investigate the case.

There was obviously a certain inclination on the part of many professional men to distance themselves from the strange goings-on at Llanfihangel-ar-arth, though there was surely only a negligible risk to their reputations. Any outcome to the investigation, whether proving that Sarah was a fasting girl or a cheat, could have been turned to their advantage. In reality, only the Jacob family had anything to lose.

The watch quickly proved to be a comic shambles. One of the watchers, a local shopkeeper called Evan Davies, was dismissed after one day on the grounds that he was a neighbour of the Jacob family. Another was dismissed after two nights 'on account of being suspected to doze'. A third was dismissed 'on grounds of his credulity'. At least one of the watchers was accused of being drunk when on duty. However, Dr Harries Davies' nephews – one a theology student at St David's, the other a medical student in his uncle's practice – managed to stay the course. Both swore on oath that they saw nothing to indicate that Sarah had anything to eat or drink for the period of the watch, apart from three drops of water to moisten her lips. They also claimed to have commenced the watch in a sceptical frame of mind, but that their minds had been changed by what they had witnessed.

This must have been a dramatic conversion. When the medical student, James Harries Davies, was interviewed by the newspapers after barely two days of watching, he was already expressing, in distinctly unsceptical terms, his amazement at the spectacle of one of Sarah's famous fits.

Only one of the watchers leaves a thoroughly credible impression. A retired farmer of seventy-two years of age, old Tom Davies of Llynbedw, told the public meeting at the Eagle Inn, Llandyfeil on Monday 7th April, 'I did my best to find out the secret, for I believe there was some secret connected with the affair.' He was especially careful to keep his eye on Sarah's mouth, noting that the girl frequently asked for her little sister Margaret and that the sisters were very affectionate with one another, with a great deal of kissing between the pair of them.

Unlike Dr Harries Davies's medical student nephew, Old Tom Llynbedw was unconvinced by the fits Sarah suffered. He said they were no more than 'tics' and that Sarah seemed to him to be perfectly healthy. He was amused to see that whereas she was apparently too weak to turn the pages of a book, Sarah could scratch her head vigorously enough 'when she was bothered by the Nits' – their very presence a further indication of good health to the down-to-earth farmer. Tom left Lletherneuadd prepared to accept that the case was an unsolved puzzle; Sarah, he said, 'would die like other children'. But he urged her parents to let the girl 'have fair play as regards her own life', now that the family honour had been satisfied.

Over the course of the watch, Sarah's bed had needed changing much more frequently than usual. She was peeing so much that the bed had to be stripped, the sheets taken to the kitchen to be washed and dried, at least once every day. Her parents were very surprised by this. Both claimed that it was the first time Sarah had passed any water since the previous December, when shock at the death of her grandfather had caused her to lose control over her bladder. They maintained that there was only one chamber-pot in the room they shared with Sarah and that the girl never appeared to use it. They put her incontinence down to the stress of having two strange men in her room day and night.

This is a wholly plausible explanation, but the presence of other people would also have made it difficult for Sarah to sneak out of bed, for example, in order to relieve herself in the farmyard. What is perhaps stranger still is that nobody – including Dr Harries Davies and his medical student nephew – thought to question how a girl who, it was claimed, had no more than a few drops of water in several days was able to produce so much urine.

The surveillance must have taken its toll on Sarah – not to say proved a severe test of her ingenuity – but she came through it with her miraculous reputation intact. The watch itself, however, was denounced in several quarters, as 'the greatest possible mockery and farce'. Not that any of this affected Sarah's power to attract visitors. In fact, more and more people than ever were coming, as the spring weather improved and Sarah became a daily fixture in the national press. By the summer, Pencader station was advertising its newly-opened refreshments bar and, although the watch committee was officially disbanded due to lack of funds, the Welsh Fasting Girl was firmly established as a lucrative cottage industry. Sarah and many of her neighbours were making more money than ever from the pilgrims; and there is no indication that any of it went to the Infirmary.

❧

Carmarthen Weekly Reporter
Saturday 1st May 1869
THE 'WONDERFUL LITTLE GIRL'
Charge of assault against a medical man
            Weds. last: Dr PEARSON HUGHES of Llandovery appeared before Llandyssul magistrates on a charge of assault against Sarah Jacob, the daughter of Mr Evan Jacob of Pencader, known as the Welsh Fasting Girl...

❦

The Spring of 1869 was to prove a turning point in the fortunes of all those concerned with events at Lletherneuadd. On 28th April Hannah Jacob found herself in the Magistrates Court at Llandyssul bringing charges of assault against one of Sarah's early visitors – John Pearson Hughes MCS, of Llandovery, a graduate of London University and lately physician-accoucher and house surgeon at University College Hospital. Pearson Hughes' visit had been the first indication of precisely what the Jacobs were pitted against and left them with an abiding distrust of doctors which was eventually to prove calamitous.

The doctor had arrived in Llanfihangel-ar-arth a couple of weeks after Reverend Jones's letter hit the presses. With two other doctors, he had gone to the home of Evan Davies, a shopkeeper in the village and friend of the Jacobs, who would later be dismissed from the watch on the grounds that he was too friendly with the family, and asked to be taken to Lletherneuadd. According to Hannah's testimony, Dr Pearson Hughes entered the parlour and removed the glove that Sarah always wore on her left hand. He then proceeded to squeeze the little girl's hand 'very hard'. Next he demanded that she put out her tongue and when Sarah refused to do this, the doctor threatened to pull it out. Hannah said that she 'begged' Evan Davies 'to take that man out', but that when she returned to the parlour Pearson Hughes had stripped Sarah and was holding a stethoscope to her chest, shouting at her in Welsh: 'Let your breath out you wicked creature!' By now the other Jacob children had joined in the commotion and their distraught mother said she told Pearson Hughes that if she 'had £5,000 I would give it to you now to go out of the house'. In reply the doctor advised her to take a birch rod and beat her children. Then, in a final act of desecration, Dr Pearson Hughes refused to place an offering upon Sarah's breast and instead threw five shillings (equivalent in value to £10.50 in modern money) on to the bed, saying that he would not believe Hannah if she swore until she was black in the face.

The doctor's version of the day's events, which he published in a letter to the *Western Mail* after Sarah's death, are broadly in keeping with Hannah's though, perhaps predictably, less melodramatic in tone. Some of the difference in tone may be because he was able to give his evidence in English – the official language of the Welsh legal system for over 300 years – whereas Hannah's was given in translation. At least once, according to the records of the hearing, a witness protested that Hannah's words had been misinterpreted, an objection the magistrate simply brushed aside. Dr Pearson Hughes was, of course, a respectable professional gentleman. He had also brought along impressive witnesses, including Dr Herbert Davies a surgeon of Llanbythal, prepared to swear on oath that in their opinion the doctor had used no unnecessary force or roughness in his examination of Sarah. Hannah was Welsh-speaking and uneducated and she had only one witness – her eldest daughter. Nobody was very surprised when the case was dismissed.

However, the court reports afford several interesting insights into the goings-on at Lletherneuadd. Firstly, Mary Jacob's evidence, like almost everyone else's, belied the hysteria of Hannah's own testimony. She stated that she did hear her mother scream out and ask Dr Pearson Hughes to leave, but only after he had been there about half an hour – affording him ample opportunity to give Sarah a thorough examination.

Evan Davies recalled that Hannah's main concern was that the doctor was what he claimed to be, and, once satisfied on that point, she had permitted him to examine Sarah without hindrance. She had even soothed the crying child while Pearson Hughes tried to check for bedsores, saying 'Don't cry, little Sal. He is a doctor and he is going to cure you.'

Pearson Hughes, for his part, had gone to Lletherneuadd determined to prove skulduggery, and his evidence was clearly intended to discredit the entire Welsh Fasting Girl phenomenon. But in spite of this, he never claimed that he was prevented from examining Sarah by Hannah, or anyone else – except, that is, by Sarah herself.

Customarily, all the strangers who made their way to Lletherneuadd were asked to wait by the fire in the kitchen before being admitted into the presence of the Fasting Girl. According to her uncle, John Daniel, Sarah always liked 'to be made smart previous to strangers entering her bedroom'.

On his visit, too, Pearson Hughes had been asked to wait in the kitchen on the grounds that 'the little girl had to put the room in order first'. To Pearson Hughes, a multitude of sins was concealed by that phrase. And he claimed that he had therefore not been very surprised when he did finally gain admission to the parlour, to find a plate of bread and butter and half a bottle of mixture on Sarah's bed.

If this is true, and we have no reason to suppose Pearson Hughes was lying, why did nobody else, before or after, ever report seeing such a thing? If

Hannah was colluding with her daughter, then why did she – having bought Sarah time to 'prepare' the room – allow such a foolish oversight? At the very least it is possible evidence of an egregious delusion on Hannah's part. Or perhaps, if the food was there, Hannah never saw it because Sarah only brought it out after her mother had left the room – and then for the benefit of the doctor. Perhaps Sarah wanted to be found out before things went too far.

Dr Hughes was naturally interested in determining whether Sarah, who allegedly had not left her bed in seventeen months, was suffering from bedsores. He was precluded from thoroughly examining the child for himself by Sarah's mounting hysteria, but when he asked the mother about the physical condition of the girl's body, Hannah made a very surprising admission to him. She stated that she had not seen her child's back since the onset of Sarah's illness – the best part of two years ago. This seems implausible, and in his evidence Evan Davies stated that Hannah had in fact told the doctor that she hadn't seen Sarah's back in ten months, not two years – but even that is very hard to believe.

There is nothing to suggest that the little girl was in any way physically neglected and unkempt. Sarah insisted on a clean flannel nightdress every day before she greeted her visitors, and since Hannah's confinement in November 1867, Evan had made her bed up every other day, changing the linen at least three times a week.

If Sarah was being given a change of clothing as regularly as she was, is it really likely that her own mother had never once in many months seen her back? Perhaps it was Evan who kept Sarah clean, but he later stated that neither he nor his wife had had any opportunity to see the child's back since February 1867. He said that the only opportunity to do so was when he changed the bed linen, but that the operation always induced one of Sarah's famous fits and so had to be carried out as quickly as possible in order to minimise her distress.

The complete absence of bedsores on Sarah's back was the final proof, of course, that the child could not possibly have been kept supine on a wretched flax mattress for the best part of two years. A more cunning person than Hannah might have argued that the lack of pressure sores was in itself evidence of a miracle. Yet Hannah instead apparently opted for a rather lame excuse.

Or perhaps she was telling the truth. Perhaps the

parents really never did see their daughter's back because she never allowed them to. So fearful were they of prompting a fit, they never forced anything. And, while Sarah liked her dadda making the bed for her, lifting her with care, smoothing and tucking the sheets just so, she was big enough to wash herself and change her nightie every day.

Dr Pearson Hughes was convinced that Sarah had not been fasting as claimed, and was not suffering from any physical disability, but he freely admitted that he was unable to prove any conscious attempt to deceive on the part of her parents. There were many people – including Sarah's own uncle – who believed that the child was perfectly capable of leaving her bed if she chose; such visitors drew the conclusion that any dissembling took the form of self-deception on the part of Hannah and Evan rather than fraudulence.

However, there were plenty of others prepared to think ill of the Jacobs. First and foremost was the vexed question of the family's apparent financial gain from the affair. There certainly was money left at Lletherneuadd. During their fateful visit, Dr Hughes had left five shillings on the child's bed and his companion, Evan Davies, had pressed two shillings into Hannah's hand. She had held on to the money for a while, before urging Davies to place it on Sarah's chest 'where everyone puts their offerings...'

According to Evan Davies's court testimony, this exchange took place during the visit on 11th March, yet in April Hannah told a journalist from the *Carmarthen Weekly Reporter* that the family had not taken any money from visitors before 27th March 1869. Up until then, only the occasional small gift, such as a book, had been accepted. Offerings of this sort were not at all uncommon in rural areas, where the cost of medical care was prohibitive. In rural Wales the custom of 'bidding' – whereby someone would go around the village asking for donations in the event of a marriage or such like – was very prevalent. It would have been strange therefore if nobody had offered poor Sarah some coppers, or the odd sixpenny bit, placing them carefully on the sick child's bosom as a mark of respect.

Hannah's ambivalence about the gifts could betray a guilty conscience, but it could also be the product of all sorts of other factors. Hannah's own words have only survived in translation, and there is every chance that they have been misinterpreted. It is also possible that there is an element of culture clash at work here, where the innocent customs of rural practice have been misunderstood, and rendered as something more venal. Most likely of all is that Hannah was embarrassed and anxious that the number of gifts Sarah was receiving had become a main topic of gossip about the family across the valley and beyond. Evan was a proud and religious man with status in the area, occupying positions of trust, and such rumours would have been wounding to him. Several sympathetic correspondents – such as Dr Thomas Lewis of Carmarthen – went to pains to point out that the family was respectable and not so needy that they would exploit their own child, but such declarations alone did not stop the whispers.

In May the *Lancet* momentarily turned its attention away from the pitched battle it was fighting with Reverend Jones and, under the headline 'The Torpid Girl', amused itself with the money question. It examined claims that in the past few months Sarah had netted the sum of £50, equivalent to about £2,300 today and an absolute fortune to a family like Sarah's.

When Hannah, emotional, bewildered, was questioned about the issue in a foreign tongue at the Magistrates' hearing against Dr Pearson Hughes, she did her best to shrug off the insinuating tone of the inquiry. 'I cannot say how much money has been given,' she imperiously told the court, 'it is so small that I don't take notice of it.' She did say that Sarah had been given 'a heap of little books', but she added, 'I don't believe they are worth £5.'

Dr Hughes' defence counsel persisted. 'Have you received £50?' he asked. '£40? Half that amount...? Have you received £15...? Ten then...?' Hannah answered in the negative to all these questions before finally agreeing that 'Yes. I should think putting it all together from the first she has had £5.' After some thought, she added that '£5 was not much for a child to receive as presents in the course of sixteen months'.

Nobody was persuaded: £5 does indeed seem a very small amount of money, even for the six weeks or so of celebrity Sarah had enjoyed by the date of the Pearson Hughes hearing at the end of April. The true amount was probably much larger. One witness to events at Lletherneuadd reckoned that at the height of her fame, in the spring and summer of 1869, Sarah was receiving about five shillings a day, which would work out at £4-10/- (nearly £200 in today's money) over six days. We know, from numerous accounts of visits to Llethrneuadd, that many people left around two shillings or half-a-crown (equivalent to about £4.50 in current value). If there were up to six or seven people in the room at any one time and if, say, just half of them left two shillings each, it would obviously not have taken long for a large sum of money to be amassed.

Some people left considerable amounts – apart from Dr Hughes' five shillings thrown on to the bed in such an insulting fashion, there was a whole sovereign left by two ladies. Then there were the other gifts. Sarah's appearance was growing increasingly bizarre as visitors left an array of trinkets, shawls and ribbons for her.

The proud Jacobs, ever mindful of their hard-won but vulnerable respectability, would have hated being the subject of such attention. They could continue to deny strenuously the rumours or they could take steps to quell them once and for all. Evan, who later swore on oath that he had personally never taken money from any of the hundreds of visitors who came to see Sarah, confided his fears to the vicar, who took on the task of dealing with the press. It wasn't long before stories were put out that no money had been received until the strangers started coming at the end of March 1869; at least one report alleged that Sarah had been refused permission to accept any gifts at all until that time. The monetary 'trifles' accepted from visitors after that date, the *Carmarthen Weekly Reporter* was told, were intended to go 'towards the cost of the watching committee'. But the committee was soon disbanded due to lack of funds, while, as the spring gave way to summer, the visitors continued to come in ever-increasing numbers, leaving behind their sixpenny bits, picture books and ribbons.

And so the rumours continued to proliferate. All through the summer the Jacobs and the vicar were under increasing scrutiny and as the pressure on them to defend their reputations intensified, so did their insistence that anyone would be welcome to conduct a thorough investigation if they cared to.

❧

By the time that the eminent physician, Dr Robert Fowler, MD, MRCS (Edinburgh), erstwhile vice-president of the Hunterian, a learned society committed to promoting the 'Science and Practice of Medicine', paid his visit to Lletherneuadd, while on holiday at the Black Lion Hotel in Cardigan in August 1869, the private agony unfolding in the back parlour was firmly established in the public forum.

Nothing that Fowler observed when he examined Sarah in August 1869 was revelatory. Dr Thomas

Lewis of Carmarthen had made essentially the same observations in the *British Medical Journal* at the end of April: the lack of any outward signs of emaciation; the give-away rumbling and gurgling noises emitting from the girl's digestive track; the unconvincing 'fits'. The Unitarian Minister, the Reverend William Thomas, MA, had been gratified to see how plump and healthy Sarah was, but confessed to having been disturbed by the 'peculiar' way her eyes had 'kept ogling us continually'. In common with others, he had noted that the child's 'voice was shrill and her utterance rapid'.

However, where all of these other gentlemen had been prepared to keep an open mind, Fowler was prepared to make a diagnosis. To him it was clear that Sarah's entire repertoire – the fainting fits, the feigned enervation, the rapid eye movements, the inability to swallow, the panicky voice – were all commonplace indications of 'simulative hysteria'.

Coupled with the bizarre dress and circus-like atmosphere at the farmstead, the whole spectacle made a 'most unfavourable, and... most suspicious' impression on a serious medical man like Fowler. Following his examination of Sarah – fairly extensive, although he was not permitted to see her back – he pronounced the child to be in 'the very perfectness of health'. As far as he was concerned, the only remarkable thing about Sarah was that she was a young girl in whom 'the propensity to deceive [was] very strongly developed'.

Fowler was very sympathetic to the 'poor simple parents' whose wholehearted belief that Sarah was miraculous was, as far as he was concerned, utterly self-evident. Fowler felt strongly that Sarah should be admitted to a hospital where she would be quickly cured of her malady. Once there, food would have been given to her via rubber tubing inserted into her bowels or up her nose.

Pitifully, Evan Jacob had responded to Fowler's suggestion by asking, 'How can you London doctors make my child eat without making a hole in her?' The doctor concluded that to leave her in the oppressive atmosphere of Lletherneuadd:

> ...an object of curiosity, sympathy and profit is not only totally antagonistic to this girl's recovery, but also renders it extremely difficult for a medical man to determine how much of the symptoms is the result of a morbid perversion of will, and how much is the product of intentional deceit.

Dr Fowler's letter, which he signed 'Observator', was printed in the *South Wales Press*, copied into the London *Times* (and almost every other newspaper published in England and Wales) and produced a furore. The reasoned and (for the time) enlightened medical opinion it proffered should have provided a much-needed chink of lucidity in the murky half-light of delusion, rumour and incomprehension that had settled around Sarah.

Fowler's suggestion that there might be a psychological basis to eating disorders, as demonstrated by behaviour such as Sarah's, was radical stuff and ultimately led to his assured reputation as one of the identifiers of 'anorexia nervosa', within the decade following Sarah's death. As it turned out, however, his intervention would serve only to seal the little girl's fate. And not because her parents would never suffer their little Sal to be taken to a faraway infirmary – the nearest was fourteen miles away – in order to be force-fed. The greatest controversy and the ensuing catastrophe stemmed from Fowler's fatal (for Sarah) error of bringing politics into the whole affair. He wrote:

> **'During the last Parliamentary Session we
> heard a great deal of the influence of the ministers**

of religion and of the power of the territorial aristocracy in Wales. Now, here is a common ground on which the eloquence of the former, and the persuasiveness of the latter, may very legitimately conjoin so as to beneficially affect a suffering fellow creature...'

In response, a leader in the *Lancet* in early April 1869 set out the issues raised by the case of the Welsh Fasting Girl once and for all. The claims made for Sarah, the leader stated, could be attributed to 'the credulity of Welsh persons', but they could be bona fide. If it were to be proved that Sarah Jacob was indeed starving herself yet somehow remaining alive, then the case was clearly 'of great importance to the medical faculty'.

While men of science pondered the implications of this point, the jibe at the expense of Welsh people did not go unnoticed either. It was later argued that Sarah had been exploited by those anxious to free, once and for all, 'the ignorant Welsh mind from the trammels of superstition and darkness'. It is certainly the case that much of the press coverage – especially that in the pages of the *Lancet* – betrayed a distinctly anti-Welsh bias. The 'strange case in Camarthenshire', already a pitched battle in the war between reason and superstition, now became a rallying point for Welsh national pride. And so it was that large and complex matters all somehow coalesced in the mystery of the little girl who lay, allegedly paralysed down the left side, mutely turning her head away when offered food or drink, reading her Bible, writing her poetry and receiving the offerings of pilgrims.

Many Welsh readers, already outraged at the way the case had provided an opportunity for the English press and establishment to, yet again, mock and deride their nation, saw in the *Lancet* leader a challenge that could not go unanswered.

None responded with more fervour than *Gohebydd* (Welsh for The Correspondent). Otherwise known as John Griffiths, *Gohebydd* was a regular contributor to the nationalistic Welsh press and a leading light of the Congregationalist movement. He was also 'London Welsh' and therefore part of the thrusting, ambitious Welsh middle class. Fiercely proud of his nation and its history, he was also determined to see *Cymru* realise its potential in the modern era.

A persuasive and passionate communicator, at the height of his powers in his late forties, he had visited Sarah in April after reading about her in the newspapers, and had left her half-a-crown. Now he determined to return to Lletherneuadd once more, in order to lead the fray in the battle for the nation's pride.

Evan Jacob responded positively to *Gohebydd*; he was probably impressed that such a celebrity was interested in him and shared his sense of persecution. It proved relatively easy for the writer to convince him of the need for a second watch. Reverend Jones had, in any case, been mooting for a more thorough investigation since the ignominious decline of the first watch back in March.

Evan told *Gohebydd* that he 'should be glad to have nurses or anything to clear his character'; he was desperate that the world should know that his 'family had always been quiet and honest and never charged with any falsehood'. With the backing of the Jacobs secured, *Gohebydd* spent the next few months writing letters to the *Baner* newspaper calling for a renewed scrutiny of Sarah's claims – one that would end the controversy once and for all.

This time any watch placed over Sarah Jacob would be untainted with charges of bias, corruption and amateurism. Moreover, it would right wrongs, absolve the innocent from shame and restitute the honour of Wales. He also wrote to his fellow Welshman, Dr J. J.

Phillips, assistant physician accoucher of Guy's Hospital in London requesting trained nurses to assist in a watch.

‧₰₰‧

1. It would be advisable, before taking any steps in the matter, to obtain a written legal guarantee from the father of Sarah Jacob sanctioning the necessary proceedings.

2. That the duty of the nurses shall be to watch Sarah Jacob with a view to ascertain whether she partakes of any kind of food, and at the end of a fortnight to report upon the case before the local committee in Carmarthenshire, and, if required, at Guy's Hospital.

3. That two nurses shall be constantly awake and on the watch in the girl's room, night and day.

4. It would be advisable for the nearest medical practitioner to watch the progress of the case; and it will be absolutely necessary for him to be prepared against any serious symptoms of exhaustion, super-veiling on the strict enforcement of the

watching, and to act according to his judgment.

5. That the room in which the girl sleeps shall be bared of all unnecessary furniture, and all possible places in the room for the concealment of food shall be closed and kept under the continual scrutiny of the watchers.

6. That if considered desirable by the local medical practitioner, or by the nurses, the bedstead on which the girl now lies shall be replaced by a single iron one.

7. That the bed on which the parents now sleep, in Sarah Jacob's room, shall be given up absolutely to the nurses.

8. That the parents be not allowed to sleep in the same room as the girl; that if they cannot at all times be prevented from approaching her, they should be previously searched (their pockets and other recesses of clothing as well as the interior of their mouths); and that no wetted towels or other such articles be allowed to be used about the girl by the parents, or any other person save the nurses; that the children of the family, and in fact every other person whatever (except the nurses), have similar restraints put upon them.

9. That the nurses have the sole management of preparing the room, bed, and patient, prior to the commencement of the watching.

10. That, as it is asserted the action of the bowels and bladder is entirely suspended, special attention must be directed to these organs.

Dr J.J. Phillips, Guy's Hospital

On 6th November 1869 the *British Medical Journal* announced the decision of Guy's Hospital to send trained nurses to Lletherneuadd, 'to watch the girl who has lately been the cause of so much curiosity'; and, the *Journal* continued – unable to resist the opportunity for a sly dig – 'expose the imposition in which she has been so long encouraged.'

Gohebydd visited the Jacobs on 23rd November, assuaging their concerns that they were in for yet more humiliation. He was evidently persuasive, for the conversation soon moved on to the conditions set for the watch. The most significant of these was the decision to replace Sarah's old cupboard bed with a simple iron bedstead. It would, of course, be much harder for her to hide food in such a bed and any lingering doubts about the parents' motivations are surely dispelled when considering how trusting they were, and that they conceded, without hesitation, to such a fundamental change in Sarah's circumstances. Indeed, the only condition set by Evan and Hannah was that one of the nurses should be a Welsh girl.

A week later the vicar chaired a meeting of thirty or forty local tradesmen and farmers at the Eagle Inn in Llanfihangel-ar-arth. Also present were Sarah's parents, her uncle, John Daniel, the solicitor of the Jacobs' landlord, and two Welsh celebrities, *Gohebydd* and *Gwilym Marles*. The presence of the latter shows the extent to which the Welsh Fasting Girl had become a focus for radical young Welsh nationalists, eager to keep stoking the passions aroused by the scandal of the Welsh evictions. *Gwilym Marles* was an impassioned and fiery orator, in the great Welsh tradition, and a champion of Welsh rights. His presence on the platform gave a strong signal to one and all that the Welsh Fasting Girl's fate and that of her nation were now one and the same.

Reverend Jones opened the meeting with a reiteration of his belief that, although there was no deceit on Sarah's part, the simple question of, 'Was the girl fed or not?' needed to be answered. *Gohebydd* presented

Dr Phillips's ten-point plan for the conduct of the watch, asserting that the adoption of these measures would satisfy that curiosity and put an end, once and for all, to the speculation in the press. Evan made only one amendment to the proposed plan: he insisted that after nine o'clock the watch be carried out in silence in order that Sarah could sleep. He sincerely hoped that the new watch would finally put an end to the accusations that had been 'thrown at his teeth'. Hannah won a round of applause with her spirited assertion that her character 'was as good as anyone's from Llanfihangel-ar-arth to London'. Then Evan signed the legal agreement.

It was decided to invite seven doctors from the area to form a medical committee responsible for supervising the watch. Dr Thomas Lewis, Mr James Rowlands, his son Mr Daniel Rowlands, Mr John Hughes, Dr George J. Hearder, Mr J. Jones and Dr Charles Caeser Corsellis were all approached. Only one of the men, Mr J. Jones, refused. Another, Mr John Hughes, made the suggestion that Sarah be seen by the same medical man each day, so that her condition could be monitored more effectively for any signs of deterioration. For, he noted, 'she may die during this trial.'

The four nurses arrived on the morning of Wednesday 8th December 1869. Big crowds turned out to see them at the stations they passed through en route from Paddington to Pencader. *Gohebydd* himself was there to meet the women at Carmarthen, where the largest crowd of all had gathered. After spending the night at lodgings, he took them to Lletherneuadd and there, at two o'clock the next afternoon, they met the family, the medical committee, the vicar, *Gwilym Marles*, and Sarah's uncle. Sarah was in good spirits and good health, 'her countenance was very sweet', observed Dr Lewis. She was wearing an embroidered nightdress and a white woollen shawl fastened with a brooch. Her hair had been fixed with a comb, atop of which sat a pink velvet bow and two yellow ribbons streamed down either side of her pretty face. A silk bonnet decorated with a wreath completed the effect. Sarah took one look at the nurses and declared at once, 'They look very kind women and I don't think they will do me any harm.' Hannah had placed a flax mat on the floor next to Sarah's bed in an effort to make the gloomy little room as homely as possible for the nurses. It was now deepest winter and the back parlour was so cold the nurses could see their own breath; Hannah had made up the new bed with a woollen counterpane and a blanket, and placed a jar of hot water at Sarah's feet.

The four nurses promptly set about the task of examining the room, its furniture and Sarah. Hannah helped to undress the little girl and watched intently as the nurses carried out the first thorough examination Sarah had undergone in over two years – even her armpits and hair were searched. Throughout the whole ordeal the child was calm and co-operative, but Hannah was frequently close to hysteria and cried out piteously in Welsh, 'Oh my child, my child, my dear little Sal! Don't do her any harm! Don't hurt her!'

Elizabeth Clinch, the sister-nurse in charge of the others, was very surprised to find that Sarah had no bedsores, especially when she considered the flock mattress the child was lying on. It was a miserable object, lumpy and hard, the ropes of the sacking it was made from easily discernible through the stained ticking cover. The nurses promptly demanded it be replaced with something more comfortable. After sister-nurse Clinch and the Welsh-speaking nurse, Anne Jones, had remade the bed, the Jacobs' own bed was removed piece by piece and an exhaustive search made of it. Nothing was found anywhere in the room to arouse suspicion, except for an old shrivelled turnip that was lying under the parents' bed. Then Sarah was examined by the doctors and pronounced quite well; she told them that she had 'no pain anywhere if not touched'.

The watches were carried out by alternate pairs of nurses in shifts of eight hours each, 2pm – 10pm, 10pm – 6am, and 6am – 2pm. Sister-nurse Clinch took the Welsh-speaking nurse Jones as her companion and kept a careful record of all that happened in a note-book that became so damp in the freezing parlour that the ink ran across its sodden pages. The first night she noted that Sarah fell asleep at just after eight o'clock, happy to be left alone with the 'nice ladies'. As she slept, Clinch observed, the little girl kept her left arm under the covers, close to her side.

The next morning the other two nurses washed Sarah and combed her hair. Evan supported his daughter in her refusal to have the back of her neck scrubbed, but the little girl was otherwise very co-operative and didn't succumb to one of her fits. In fact, she never had a fit again. Sarah spent most of the first day reading and being read to by sister-nurse Clinch, which she liked very much. No doctors came to visit, but the nurses were content that she was well and happy, although the second night she was far more restless than the first.

At 5.30am on the third day of the watch the nurses noticed that Sarah was very wet. Her night-dress was soaked and there were three 'crown-sized' excrement stains (a crown was a coin the size of a 50 pence piece) on the back of it. According to Evan this was the first time that Sarah had passed any urine since the previous August, when the death of the family cow had an adverse and uncommon effect upon her bladder control.

Her bladder and bowels now emptied, and over the next twenty-four hours Sarah began to weaken dramatically. By the time sister-nurse Clinch took her turn at 2pm on the Saturday afternoon she noticed that Sarah's distinctively strong voice was markedly weaker. Concerned, she asked Sarah if she wanted anything. Sarah said no.

Although she continued to refuse food, in other respects Sarah exhibited a great deal of trust in the nurses. She liked them and they liked her: she was, they all agreed, a very sweet and affectionate little girl. 'Kissey me, kissey me,' she would say to sister-nurse Clinch. The Jacobs shared their daughter's trust in the nurses and were gratified to see how kind the women were to the little girl. Throughout the entire ordeal they assiduously observed their side of the bargain and left most of the task of caring to Sarah to the nurses. They never went near to the bed, although Evan was always present when it was being made.

The anxiety of Evan and Hannah was palpable. They came into the room frequently. On more than one occasion Hannah could be seen peering in through the little window above where Sarah lay. The nurses noted that whereas both parents were very fond and affectionate towards the girl, Evan was especially so. Every day he would ask her how she was and every day he would receive the answer he must have come to dread: 'Just the same, dadda.'

On the fourth day of the watch, Sunday 12th December, Mr Hughes paid a visit in the afternoon. Evan refused to give him permission to check under the bedclothes, but Hughes was able to carry out routine checks. He noticed that Sarah's pulse was much higher but he wasn't unduly concerned. That night, as sister-nurse Clinch watched over her, Sarah was increasingly restless. She was not the only one to find sleep difficult. As the nurse half-dozed in a chair near the door of the freezing parlour, her feet covered with warm flannel and resting on a stone hot-water bottle, she was aware that one of Sarah's sisters was moving about in the kitchen. After a while the girl lay down on the settle, where she appeared to sleep until 2am. Then, in the flickering half-light of the candle, the nurse could discern the shadows the girl made as she moved restlessly about the room before throwing herself onto a chair. After a little while she opened the door to the farmyard, then she went off to sleep in the children's bedroom. Was this evidence of a sister's last-ditch, futile attempt to help Sarah either fetch food or go out to the farmyard to relieve herself?

When Sarah woke at 5.30 it was observed that once again her nightdress was wet. The child seemed confused as the nurses changed the soaking bed linen, and unaware that she had wet herself during the night. Her father asked the nurses not to say anything to her but, when questioned later, Sarah told the nurse that she never had any idea when she wanted to pee.

At 8pm that evening the nurse noticed a bad smell and, on examining the bed, found that Sarah had wet herself yet again. She had also managed to pull the cork out of her hotwater bottle, and the whole bed had to be exchanged for another. While this was being done, Sarah appeared to her father to be going into one of her fits, but the sensible nurse knew better. She asked Sarah bluntly if it was true – was she really about to lose control of her faculties? The girl apparently knew when she had met her match: she opened her eyes immediately and answered in the negative. Moreover, she went straight to sleep in the new bed that was found for her, something Evan had said she would never do.

Was Sarah trying to prise the cork from the stone water bottle, in a last desperate effort to quench what must have been by then an unbearable thirst? Does the dark groove found on her big toe in the autopsy tell its own story? Sarah may have been – surely must have been – desperate, but she was not going to betray herself. As a result, she was very much worse on the Tuesday. Her eyes were sunken and the pupils dilated; her voice was very weak.

After she had been awake reading for a couple of hours, the rope tying the sacking to her bedstead snapped and this time her water bottle crashed on to the floor. Sarah went into a real faint, but when she came to, she was able to laugh about what had happened. She was far from well, though, and when the vicar came to visit her that afternoon, he was shocked by the deterioration in her looks and spirit. Her pulse was fast and she was very pale, yet when he visited a short while later, Dr Harries Davies was insistent that there was 'no indication of danger'.

Mr Hughes and Mr Rowlands came in the afternoon, but Sarah kept the blankets up to her chin, refusing to let the doctors see beneath them and Evan again refused to leave them alone with her, on the grounds that 'another doctor had once used her very roughly'. By now Sarah's pulse was racing, but both doctors left without drawing any conclusions. When they had gone the nurses noticed that Sarah had passed a small amount of urine.

That night, sister-nurse Clinch later reported, they detected a strange, fetid smell about the bed 'not like the usual smell of death, and I cannot describe what it was like'. Sarah was very cold too and her mother warmed her own flannel petticoats to place over her little daughter.

By 10pm Sarah was gulping air. The strange smell, it was later ascertained, was the peculiar pear-drop-like smell of ketosis, the so-called 'odour of sanctity', a common occurrence in cases of prolonged fasting. The constant gaping was a sign of acute air hunger. The nurses had seen many people die before, but never, they later admitted, of starvation.

On Wednesday, Sarah was still strong enough to refuse to let Mr John Hughes examine her, though she did let the nurses have a look at her. She also asked for a little eau de Cologne on a handkerchief from one of them. When Dr Lewis came to see her, he was satisfied that she was not in any immediate danger. But her parents were worried enough to ask the nurses not to change her linen anymore, believing that this was the cause of Sarah's discomfort. All the while, visitors continued to arrive at the stricken farmhouse – though, as one of the nurses observed, none of them left any money.

The doctors spoke to Evan that day, but gave him no indication that there was any serious cause for alarm. Nurse Attrick later stated that Dr Lewis had actually told her not to worry, on the grounds that Sarah's parents had seen her worse many times before. But by the early morning of Thursday 16th December Sarah was gravely ill and her parents and sister-nurse Clinch were very worried. The child's nose was pinched, her cheekbones very prominent, her eyes sunken. She was parched and exceedingly pale. The curious smell emitting from her was worse than ever.

Reverend Jones, fearing the worst, pleaded with her parents to tell the nurses to leave. Perhaps Evan might have heeded the vicar's words, as he had many times before, if Dr Harries Davies had not assured them all that Sarah was in no danger.

In fact, although the doctor said this, as soon as he left Lletherneuadd he went straight to Sarah's uncle in Pencader and told him to go immediately and talk some sense into Evan. Then he wired Dr Lewis in Carmarthen. In the record-book he wrote that he did all of this because of 'a little anxiety on the part of the sister-nurse'; yet it seems that he was the one who was more than a little anxious.

Sarah's uncle, John Daniel, arrived at Lletherneuadd about 2pm, to find that Sarah had rallied a little. He talked to her about a picture Dr Corsellis had sent her which was now sitting on the mantelpiece, but when Daniel suggested to his niece that she might like a drop of water, Sarah closed her eyes and turned her head away. As Nurse Attrick said later, it was obvious that 'she was not pleased' by the suggestion.

Evan was surprised to see his brother-in-law and was astonished when John Daniel told him that he was there under doctor's orders, having been informed that Sarah was in grave danger. Evan, who had been told by the same doctor a few hours earlier that there was no cause for concern, threatened to kick his brother-in-law out of the house for interfering.

At four o'clock Dr Lewis and John Hughes came to visit, but Hannah refused to let Mr Hughes in, adamant that 'only Dr Lewis shall see her'. Mr Hughes replied, 'Never mind Lewis. Go in if the girl is ill or dying. I don't want to see her.' But Sarah herself agreed to let him in to give a second opinion.

It was dark in the room and Hughes was unable to see Sarah's face, but he took her pulse: it was 160. He admitted to his colleague that he was very frightened and the two doctors told Evan that the watch should be withdrawn immediately and some food offered to Sarah. Evan replied that he wished the nurses to continue the watch, and that he would not offer his daughter any food because he had made a vow two years ago to do that only if she asked for some.

Hughes went home and resigned from the medical committee that very night. Lewis, however, remained in attendance and was joined by Dr Harries Davies later that evening. Both doctors appear to have convinced themselves that all their earlier fears and those of their colleague were an overreaction. The excessive rate of Sarah's pulse was not as alarming as Hughes had made it out to be, after all: there was 'no clamminess of the skin, no delirium, no disturbance of the intellect'. Sarah was even able to talk with Lewis. She was, she told him, looking forward to having her photograph taken so that she could give a copy to each of the nurses. Nurse Jones, however, reported that she thought Sarah was wandering in her speech: she couldn't understand what the little girl was saying to her, or even if she was speaking Welsh or English. She told the Jacobs, 'If she were mine I would give her a drop of brandy and water in a spoon', to which Hannah replied, 'We have made an oath not to offer her anything.'

When sister-nurse Clinch came back on duty at 10pm she was not at all surprised to find that Sarah was very much worse. There was a strong smell of eau de Cologne permeating the room and Sarah was very delirious. She repeatedly called for her parents, but when Evan came to her, she told him, 'Run out father and shut the door.' As soon as the poor man was out of the room she would call for him again. Her mother asked her 'How are you little Sal?', but little Sal told her, 'You go out and shut the door.' Her big sister Mary came in and was sent away again. Evan told her that whatever she wanted she should have, but he was careful not to mention either food or water. Warm flannels were applied to her feverish little body, but nothing helped, and Evan confided in Nurse Jones that he expected Sarah to die. As the night wore on, she became so restless that it was necessary to bring in bolsters to keep her from falling out of the bed.

At 3am on Friday 17th December Sarah called out one last time. Evan immediately came to her and in trying to make her comfortable, retrieved a bottle of eau de Cologne, which had gone missing the day before, from underneath her left arm. Evan was stunned – he had never known Sarah to conceal anything before.

With the discovery, Sarah seemed to lose all hope of survival and began to relinquish her hold on life. She was pitifully cold and, at Evan's suggestion, her little sister Margaret was brought into the room and put into bed naked beside her, but this time the method that had proved so beneficial in the past had no effect. Nurse Jones told the parents that in her opinion Sarah was dying and the rest of the Jacob children came into the room to kiss her goodbye. At 5am Dr Harries Davies was sent for but, after some discussion with Evan, he decided not to give the child anything.

In the final hours of Sarah's life on Friday 17th December nothing further was done to save her. When her uncle John Daniel arrived that afternoon he immediately saw that his niece was dying and he begged Evan to moisten the child's lips. 'I cannot do that,' said Evan, 'as I gave permission to Dr Harries Davies to do so and he wouldn't.'

Daniel told his wife to wipe the girl's lips with his own handkerchief. Soon after this was done, at about 3pm, just as the light dropped from the winter sky, Sarah died.

⁂

'THE WELSH FASTING GIRL IS DEAD'
Telegram sent to the Carmarthen Weekly Reporter and reprinted on every newspaper billboard in London.

n

Poor murdered girl. I was sure the doctors would finish her off when they got her into their hands... The sudden plunging of her into the adverse influences of a posse of doctors and nurses, the majority of whom were filled with suspicion of her and hostility to her... was... like being plunged and kept down in an atmosphere of carbonic acid gas...
content of a letter sent to
W.M. Wilkinson, solicitor to Evan Jacob, Jan 1870.

It was not necessary for the coroner to send for Evan. He went of his own accord to the New Inn where the inquest into Sarah's death was convened at 12 o'clock, on Tuesday 21st December 1869. Just an hour before, the jury had assembled at Lletherneuadd to view the body, which Sarah's maternal grandfather, who lived nearby, had just positively identified. Evan put his side of the story clearly, unfaltering, with no trace of high emotion.

He was, he stated, never made aware by the medical people that his daughter was in danger of dying of starvation. He believed her to be incapable of taking food, though he could not say how it was that she had survived so long without. If anyone had made it clear to him that Sarah was dying for want of food, he would not have refused her access to any.

The Coroner dismissed his testimony as 'hideous nonsense'. After deliberating for fifteen minutes, on the afternoon of Thursday 23rd December the Coroner recommended a verdict of manslaughter, which carried a maximum penalty of life imprisonment, against the parents. Evan and Hannah were formally arrested and bound over to reappear before the

THE ILLUSTRATED
POLICE  NEWS
LAW COURTS AND WEEKLY RECORD.

FRIDAY, DECEMBER 24, 1869.

THE LAST HOURS OF THE WELSH FASTING GIRL

Llandyssul magistrates in two months time. They returned to Lletherneuadd to attend to the funeral arrangements for Sarah, whose body still lay on the little truckle bed in the back parlour.

That night the last evening train, the same which five days earlier had spread the news of her death along the line to Carmarthen and beyond, broke down near Llanpumpsaint with the Coroner and reporters on board, and a new one had to be sent for from Carmarthen. Meanwhile, Sarah's family and neighbours gathered in the kitchen around the little coffin, placed on an impromptu bier made up of chairs draped in white cloth (for a virgin), for the customary *wyl nos* – night of tears.

In the course of the long night's vigil, in the shadows cast by the two solitary candles placed either side of the coffin, did they speculate on how she might have deceived them all? Were there tearful confessions from her sisters or little brothers? Was the enveloping silence ripped by howls of remorse and regret from her parents? Had anyone, apart from the fairies, seen Sarah tiptoe into the dairy? Could they, any of them, imagine her filling up her little bottle with milk from the pails, breaking off a little piece of bread, sipping a spoonful of cawl from the saucepan, gobbling up the remains of the fish her dadda or brother had caught in the river? Deceiving them all...

Or was it easier simply to carry on believing in the miracle? How they must have wondered that night, and in all the years to come, what she might have become, what sort of woman she would have grown to. If only she had been left alone.

※

On Monday 28th February 1870, the members of the medical committee, the eight local doctors who had devised and supervised the final watch over Sarah Jacob, were arraigned, along with her parents before the Llandyssul magistrates. For nine days the evidence of an array of witnesses was heard in English.

Hannah sat through it all, close to the fire, her shawl pulled tight about her, seemingly oblivious to everything, rocking to and fro and moaning piteously to herself. Evan was beside her, ramrod straight, his chiselled features an impenetrable mask of gravity concealing whatever turmoil his soul was in. From time to time he would reach across to gently pat his wife's back, or whisper a few soothing words in her ear, comforting her as best he could. After a half-hour deliberation, the charges against the doctors were dropped and Evan and Hannah were sent to trial at the mid-summer assizes in Carmarthen. Their case was set for July 12th 1870. They were admitted to bail to the immense sum of £100 and two sureties of £50 each (£100 being equivalent to £4700 in current value).

Few in Welsh society were surprised when the medical men (three of whom were magistrates themselves) were not committed for trial alongside Evan and his wife, but the committal of Sarah's parents resulted in a spate of intense speculation in England. The *Law Times* devoted many column inches in the months between the magistrates' hearing and the trial to debate the wider ethical implications of the case.

Had Sarah died from 'nervous excitement', resulting from the strain of being 'watched' for the last week of her life? If so, then who could be held responsible for the 'wicked experiment'? The parents in permitting their child to starve to death, or the doctors who had failed to induce her to eat? Was there any imperative in law to force an unwilling child to take food? If so, did failure to force-feed constitute an act of criminal negligence and, in such an event, where would the responsibility ultimately lie?

Very few commentators accepted that Sarah had been the victim of her parents' greed. Even the

London *Times*, which had long been scornful of the case and the Jacobs in particular, lay much of the blame for the tragic outcome at the feet of the medical profession. Evan Jacob, after all, was no more than an ignorant peasant who obviously shared his daughter's 'disturbed mental state'; no such excuse, however, could be made for the professional men who allowed an 'unhappy girl... to exist for two whole years in a state of prolonged hysterical simulation'.

Whereas just two months earlier it had been easy to find plenty of commentators prepared to keep an open mind about the veracity of Sarah's claims, thereby stimulating public interest in the case, by February 1870 there had been a great sea-change. Most people now were of the opinion that Sarah had been in the grip of hysteria. She was a deranged and duplicitous child, who had the misfortune to be surrounded by gullible fools and incompetent medical men.

Dr. Fowler had caused a sensation when called as an expert witness at the magistrates' hearing. It was his considered opinion that Sarah was 'a night-feeder', who either 'thought she could outwit the nurses, as she had previously outwitted the first set of watchers; or had got herself into that state of mind in which she believed she could last out the fortnight without food.'

How could she have known that after just one week without eating or drinking, the will to survive of even the strongest man becomes severely weakened?

The parents were absolved of all blame in the matter in Dr Fowler's account, because he was in the vanguard of those who placed the responsibility firmly on Sarah herself; but there were many others who looked to the doctors involved for an explanation.

With the clarity of hindsight and the advantages of almost 150 years of steady progress in medical science and practice, it seems as if Henry Harries Davies acted in a grossly negligent way throughout the entire course of Sarah's illness. His lack of experience and plain common sense was apparent from the very first instance of Sarah's strange illness in February 1867 right up to her death in December 1869. He was too eager to take the parents' lead, allowing himself to be influenced by them in the way the case was diagnosed and handled.

But the medical profession in the 1860s was a new entity, and medical practice was often rudimentary and still heavily dependent on ancient wisdoms and techniques – herbal cures, enemas, powders and blood-letting. Many doctors were afraid to adopt modern methods lest they alienate their patients, and many shared their patients' scepticism towards, and even fear of, the imprecision of medical science. Let us not forget, too, that Harries Davies was caught up in the mystery and romance surrounding the wonderful little girl; like Sarah's parents and the Reverend Jones, he wanted to believe.

On the afternoon of her last day, as Sarah lay dying, Dr Harries Davies finally asked Evan's permission to give the little girl some brandy and water. In his testimony, he alleged that the father was adamant that Sarah was unable to swallow anything: 'It will kill her,' he told the doctor. He told the magistrate that he reasoned the parents had seen Sarah close to death many times before; he believed that they knew the case better then he did. Therefore, in his mind, the final responsibility rested with the father.

Evan also recalled the desperate conversation, held at the back-parlour door, but in his version of events Harries Davies had asked him – Evan – to administer the restorative. Evan admitted that he had been unable to bring himself to do this, so convinced had he been, for so long by then, that the act of swallowing would kill Sarah. He could not bear the thought that he would have the weight of his daughter's death on his conscience as a consequence of something he had done, but he did defer to the doctor's professional opinion and gave him permission to feed Sarah if he wished. The doctor entered the back parlour intending so to do. When he re-emerged a few minutes later, Evan asked him if he had offered Sarah anything. A look passed between the two men, and the doctor admitted that he hadn't. Poised at the little girl's bedside with the restorative in hand, he had panicked. He told Evan, 'I was afraid that she had been so long without food she would choke.'

❧

I did not say it was possible; I only said it was true
Sir Astley Cooper (1768-1841), President of the
Royal College of Surgeons, Surgeon to George IV,
William IV and Queen Victoria. *Quoted by W.M.
Wilkinson, Esq., Defence lawyer for Evan Jacob*

❧

Evan Jacob's solicitor, W. M. Wilkinson, immediately started a campaign to raise funds for the trial to be heard in London where expert witnesses could be more easily summoned, and where his client would be far away from what he denounced as the inevitable 'mockery, delusion and snare' of a Welsh jury. Wilkinson, well aware that the Welsh establishment had been embarrassed by the Fasting Girl case and was still stinging from the blows administered by the English press, knew that a fair trial was out of the question. The respectable, educated medical men involved in the case would not be challenged in a Welsh court, no matter how much the London lawyers clamoured for them to answer to some of the charges being put in the journals. The ancient superstitions, and stubborn monoglotism of the remote uplands would be held to account for this scandal: Evan Jacob alone would bear the brunt.

Wilkinson received several small cheques to help him defend Evan and prosecute the cruel indifference of Empiricism and Dry Reason. One man offered £100, but Wilkinson was reluctant to take such a large amount out of one pocket, 'where the duty lies on so many to give Science a fair trial'. Instead he published a pamphlet at his own expense, which put Evan's case and presented many examples of 'asitia and deposis' – lengthy fastings that had not resulted in death. Alongside these was a disquisition on the numerous instances of live toads apparently springing forth from inside the rocks and boulders where they had long been incarcerated. Wilkinson also collected the opinions of several doctors and scientists, all agreeing that Sarah's death was caused by the 'excitement of being watched', and many verifying the notion that it was possible to live without sustenance. This, then, constituted the basis of the case for the defence.

The trial lasted a week and, despite the urgent need for it to be conducted in London, took place in Camarthen, commencing on 12th July 1870. The fate of the Jacobs twisted and writhed like an eel. To begin with, many had believed that, with the doctors out of the picture, there was no case to answer whatsoever and that the case would be dropped before it even came to trial. And that, even if, against all the odds, the trial did proceed, then surely a jury of ordinary Welsh people would support the parents?

The popular consensus was to be proved wrong on both counts. From the outset, the Judge took the unequivocal view that parents had a legal and natural duty to ensure that their children were fed. Whatever had occurred at Lletherneuadd in the months before, Sarah Jacob had died because her parents, in the days leading up to her death, had neglected 'to supply her with the food which she had previously received'. The Grand Jury had no choice, in such a clear-cut case of parental neglect, but to proceed to a full trial. And this they duly did. Hannah and Evan Jacob were to be tried with 'having feloniously killed and slain one Sarah Jacob at Lletherneuadd on the 17th December 1869'. The charge was put to them in Welsh. They both pleaded not guilty.

The prosecution case rested on the understanding that Sarah – having suffered a 'fit of hysterics' – really was able to exist on very little food. She colluded with her parents in developing a little trickery, harmless at first, in order to bring much-needed cash to the parents and satisfy the need for attention of a pretty, clever and vain little girl. Instead of telling their friends and neighbours that Sarah was living on very little – which would not have been so remarkable in a place where hardly anybody ate very well – the family made the more impressive claim that the girl was able to live on nothing at all. They never intended for the ruse to go as far as it did. They certainly never expected that Sarah would die as a consequence of it. But that is what happened.

'The child is dead. She was starved to death,' and Mr Giffard QC, counsel for the prosecution, was in no doubt that she had been starved to death by her own parents, in order to maintain the 'trick' they had devised.

The prosecution case never once admitted the possibility that there were many people who believed in fairies, in ghosts, in girls who could live on air, and that the defendants were among them.

Evan and Hannah were tried in a foreign language and within the framework of an entirely alien culture. Evan Jacob was a ruined and broken man. The farm he had spent almost twenty years building up had been left untended since Sarah's death. His wife – dressed in heavy mourning and unable to speak coherently – was an emotional wreck. The loss of his child was a terrible blow, but not once did Evan waver or falter in his belief that Sarah was very ill, that she really went without food and that to give her food would have killed her. That, for him, was the nub of the whole case and there was no way that he could be persuaded to look at the terrible events in any other way.

There were no witnesses prepared to swear on oath that they had ever seen Evan (or anyone else) give Sarah anything to eat or drink; but more crucially there was nobody to suggest how this little girl had persisted single-handedly in her duplicity for so long. Evan and Hannah were hard at work all day, and were absent from the farmstead for long periods, but there were others in the household who were present at least some of the time. Yet neither the prosecution nor defence called any of the Jacob children, or the manservant, as witnesses. Under oath, at least one of them may have been persuaded to tell the truth in defence of the parents, to let slip some revealing observation or offer some tangible proof of their innocence. As it was, Evan's fundamental belief in Sarah went unchallenged; there was no evidence of deceit because there had been no deceit.

In his summing up the judge commended John Hughes, the surgeon from Carmarthen who had admitted to being 'frightened' by Sarah's pulse rate, but added, 'it is very much to be regretted that he did not take more active steps than he did.' However, he focused his directions to the jury upon Evan and Hannah Jacob's failure to supply Sarah with food over the last few days of her life. He made it quite clear that he held them entirely responsible for the tragic outcome at Lletherneuadd, the result of 'a wicked experiment', to be sure, but one which was, to his mind, compounded by the Jacobs' apparent lack of the most basic common sense.

He found it very difficult to believe, for example, that they could have slept in the same room as Sarah for two years, yet not have known that 'she had in any way got rid of natural excreta'. If they were aware of the fact that she was emptying her bowels and bladder, then they must have known that she was eating and they were therefore guilty of a terrible deception. He directed the jury, that if the parents 'abstained from giving their child food... in order that they might not be detected in the deception which they practised by asserting that she had no food, then they are guilty of manslaughter.'

After a short deliberation, the jury returned a guilty verdict, but recommended clemency in the case of the mother 'who was under the control of her husband'. Evan declared simply: 'We are not guilty.' Hannah buried her face in her shawl and sobbed.

※

Evan was sentenced to one year's hard labour at Swansea gaol. His wife, by then pregnant with her eighth child, was sentenced to six months. A large crowd turned out to see them off from Pencader station on Tuesday 19th July 1870. Mobs are fickle and few of them would now have doubted that the couple was guilty as charged. As a local correspondent had predicted back in May 1869, Lletherneuadd, once the locus of Hannah and Evan's dreams of a comfortable and respectable future for their young family, had 'become a word synonymous with disgrace'. Until well into the 1950s, when the last of Sarah's sisters died, the inhabitants of Llanfihangel-ar-arth kept their thoughts to themselves about the story that had brought such shame to their lonely valley. As recently as 1983, the *Carmarthen Journal* published a series of articles impugning the Jacobs as inhuman exploiters of Sarah.

Evan and Hannah arrived at the forbidding stone buildings of the newly-built prison in the long hot summer of 1870 – a drought year and one of the worst for farming in living memory. They would have passed through the dark and ill-ventilated reception areas, separate ones for men and women, in the company of other felons: housebreakers, street brawlers, drunks, prostitutes. They would be checked for infectious disease and lice and then given their prison uniforms to wear, scratchy, ill-fitting and decorated with broad arrows. They would spend the months to come engaged in a series of tasks expressly designed – in accordance with the Earl of Carnarvon's 1863 Prison Bill – to 'visibly quicken the breath and open the pores'.

For Hannah that would have entailed grinding mountains of laundry through the presses, until her

Evan and Hannah Jacob, photographed for their prison record

pregnancy became too pronounced for such effort and then she would have sat picking oakum or sewing canvas bags until her fingers bled.

Evan would have been put to work breaking rocks or on the treadmill. The treadmill at Swansea gaol – a huge drum, six feet in diameter – was still in use at the end of the nineteenth century and was used to pump water. Sixty-four men at a time were set to work the wheel by climbing a great chain of steps, which drove the motion of the wheel, which in turn forced them to climb another step, and another, and another. At each a man was forced to lift his body three feet, as he covered a distance of over two thousand feet an hour – over a day the equivalent to climbing Snowdon two-and-a-half times.

Both Hannah and Evan were, of course, used to

hard work and physical privation, but how heavily the shame must have weighed upon them both. The Victorian prison system after 1864, used the Separate System, in effect solitary confinement, and the Silent System, under which prisoners had to refrain from talking to one another as they went about their tasks. Alone, in silence, there would have been plenty of time to think about everything that had happened; to worry about the children left to fend for themselves in the outside world; to grieve. Perhaps the mindless tasks they had to perform enabled them to lose themselves for a while each day. Perhaps exhaustion overtook them, numbing them, releasing them from the obsessive mental patterns of grief.

The professional men connected with the case simply returned to their lives, their careers unhindered, their reputations unimpaired. *Gohebydd*, the journalist, continued writing articles championing the Welsh cause until his death in 1877. Reverend Jones remained friends with the Jacobs, at least until he left Llanfihangel-ar-arth in 1875.

At the end of 1870 he baptised Hannah's new baby daughter, born in prison, and he recommended the Jacobs' eldest son, Evan Saunders, to his successor at the vicarage, who gave the boy much-needed employment in his service. He went on to enjoy a happy second marriage and a distinguished career as Rector of Newport. He died in 1904 and is buried in Llanfihangel-ar-arth churchyard, right by the porch door, alongside his beloved first wife and their eldest daughter.

Dr Harries Davies continued to practise in his native district until his death in 1913 at the age of seventy-seven. He is buried a short distance away from the vicar. The epitaph on his grave reads 'Glorious is the Fruit of Good Labours'.

When she came out of prison in January 1871, Hannah found a tiny cottage near the stone quarry at Penlan, a mile from Llanfihangel-ar-arth, where she lived with Esther, her youngest son David and the new baby, Hannah. The other children, including Sarah's favourite, seven-year-old Margaret, were farmed out to various neighbours and relatives, scraping some much-needed money together by working as servants.

The inhabitants of Llanfihangel-ar-arth do not appear to have shunned the family; they opted instead to carry on as if none of it had ever happened, whilst maintaining a fit and proper circumspection in regard to the matter. That is, somehow, a very Welsh reaction. We may suppose that there was gossip, plenty of it, but only among friends and neighbours, behind closed doors, over the knitting or a cup of tea.

By the time Evan Jacob left prison in July 1871, the farm at Lletherneuadd was lost to them forever, but at least the family was reunited and able to begin their slow ascent back to respectability. On the 1881 census they can be found occupying the Old Shop at New Inn, and farming thirty-two acres – the amount of land Evan had started with at Lletherneuadd almost thirty years before.

Events seem to have taken their toll on the eldest daughter, Mary, who is recorded as 'ailing', but Hannah and Evan did their best to carry on. A ninth child, Rachel, was born in 1872, and a baby, Enoch, was born in 1878 – the only one of Hannah Jacob's children to die in infancy. Within twenty years of leaving prison, Evan had progressed to farming fifty-eight acres at Crosmaen, close to the village centre of Llanfihangel-ar-arth and about a mile to the west of Lletherneuadd-uchaf.

Did they ever consider what it might have been like to have returned there, how fortunate they were not to have done so? How could they have entered the back-parlour night after night without fancying they could hear her stirring, the rustle of a page turning, perhaps, or her clear distinctive voice intoning one of her prayers or hymns? Surely they would have found themselves standing in the rapidly cooling yard at sunset, calling for her, their lost lamb, to come home? Ghosts follow us wherever we go. A guttering candle can catch the glittering of a bright eye. Waking suddenly in the endless dark night, you might just glimpse a small shadow flitting past the open door. And memory haunts – maybe even more so. A beautiful child walking across the field from Chapel, slightly apart from the others, lost in thought. A toddler in a snow-white pinafore chasing the chickens in the yard. A baby reaching out to be kissed.

But life goes on... The eldest son, Evan Saunders Jacob, married a middle-aged widow woman with whom he had a daughter and worked on farmland in the village. When his first wife died he remarried and had three more little girls. Samuel also married and farmed at Cwm Mackwith, next door to the vicarage. He had a son, Gwilym. Sarah's sister Esther died in 1891 – a spinster aged thirty-five. Her baby brother David went on to study theology at Lampeter, attaining his License of Divinity in 1893. He worked as a curate in several Glamorganshire parishes, and was the vicar of St Cadoc Bedlinog from 1912 until his death in 1917.

Evan didn't live long enough to see his son realise his full potential, but he would have been very proud of him all the same. Evan died at Crosmaen in 1895, aged sixty-three, from 'waxy liver' – a degenerative condition. He had most likely been ill for a long time with a virulent, infectious disease – probably TB – which had gone undetected and unchecked before it finally destroyed his liver. Dr Harries Davies was in attendance, and signed the death certificate.

Hannah outlived Evan by twelve years, and carried on running the farm at Crosmaen until her death. The last of her surviving children, Rachel, died in 1958 aged 85. Mary, 'ailing' in 1881, survived into her eighties and didn't pass away until 1932. Sarah's favourite sister, Margaret, whom she had loved to kiss and who had been slipped naked into bed with her as she lay dying, was still alive a few months before the outbreak of the Second World War.

All Sarah's siblings took whatever they knew with them to the grave. It is hard to believe that if any of them had ever witnessed or assisted Sarah in her subterfuge, they stood mutely by when their parents were sent to prison. Perhaps the family had made another solemn vow, as binding as that between Hannah and Evan, never to speak of the matter again, to keep it all a secret. Secrets were something at which some members of this family obviously excelled. Perhaps they all decided to keep the faith.

In his examination of the case published in 1871 Robert Fowler concluded that Sarah had been a 'night-feeder', encouraged in her deception by the 'parental coaxings, endearments, indulgences and pettings' she received in exchange for refusing the food offered to her. And this became the received wisdom – everything that happened was at the behest of a spoilt, vain, wilful and hysterical child. Few people doubted that; they only argued over the degree to which the parents were dupes, idiots or thoroughly complicit.

Many people who witnessed these events knew that Sarah could move about if she wanted to; there were plenty who saw how plump and healthy she became the longer she went without food. Only her parents failed to see what was right there before them. At first they were so frightened she would die, they did everything to keep her safe from harm; then they strove just to keep her happy. Somewhere along the line it became an act of faith, pure and simple, to believe everything she claimed. Ultimately, they simply could not bring themselves to believe that, far from being a miracle, their darling little girl was actually a liar and a cheat.

I don't suppose that they ever came to accept that. Much easier to believe that a girl could live on air. And by then they were surrounded by any number of educated and sophisticated people who believed just that. Then there was also the matter of their pride. That, as Old Tom Llynbedw had hinted, was perhaps their only real sin.

So what of the facts? Sarah Jacob had been a very sick little girl. For a few weeks in the winter of 1867 she had almost died, probably from viral encephalitis. She had taken a long while to recover, but because her mother was such a diligent and caring nurse, and because she was a strong and healthy child, she had pulled through. Perhaps she sustained some brain damage, perhaps not; but Sarah clearly emerged from her brush with death determined never to be overlooked again. She had enjoyed the attention. She was clever. Perhaps she even reasoned that she had nothing left to lose. No doubt she eventually came to believe in her own mythology, in her own supernatural power. And why wouldn't she? Everyone else did.

Is it incredible that she achieved all of this on her own? That she was so strong-willed? Remember that this was the child who, as she lay dying, almost undoubtedly tried to prise the cork out of a hotwater bottle with her toe, rather than ask a kind nurse for a drink of water – the dark pinch-marks on her toe found in the autopsy speak for themselves. Remember that in the last hours of her life her adoring father was devastated to discover an eau de cologne bottle hidden under her left arm, yet still she abjured any offer of help. On the last day of her life she somehow summoned the strength to stubbornly resist her uncle's attempts to save her. Such a person could do anything, unaided and with only the fairies as witnesses.

꙳

When I visited the graveyard at Llanfihangel-ar-arth, which stands exposed on the top of an ancient mound, it was cold and damp even though it was a warm August day. The people I spoke with in the village were more eager to talk than they might have been a few years before; they all knew about Lletherneuadd and what had happened there, but one sensed the need to tread carefully. This, after all, was their story.

One lady told me that Hannah and Evan were buried in the churchyard, but she and everyone else denied the existence of a grave or any sort of memorial to 'the little girl'. Undeterred, I searched among the long, wet grass for nearly an hour, before finding the simple stone marker, across the graveyard from the large and splendidly decorated tombs of the vicar and the doctor, in a neglected and overgrown corner on the north edge.

It looked as though it had probably been added at a later date – perhaps by Sarah's clergyman brother on a visit home – when some of the grave's inhabitants had already been laid to rest beneath the thick soil, the last layer of those who had once walked upon this corner of the earth.

The inscription on the low, gabled stone is almost worn, but you can just make out the words, '*Dy ewyllys di a weler*' – which translate as something like 'Thy will be done!'. If you lie flat on the ground, provided the sun is against you, you can also make out the names and dates of the rest of the family. In the grave with Hannah and Evan are their baby son Enoch, Esther, Sarah and her four long-lived sisters – none of whom ever married or left Llanfihangel-ar-arth.

Let us hope Sarah is sleeping soundly now; secure in the knowledge that her secret is safe with them.

ACKNOWLEDGEMENTS

Thanks are due to the staff and librarians at the British Library Newspaper Collection at Colindale. Also to my cousin Mr William Wyn Evans of Nant byr Uchaf, Ceredigion for reading early drafts, correcting my Welsh and being so generous with his knowledge of the setting and background to this story. I would also like to thank all the people at Llanfihangel-ar-arth who took time to talk to me, especially Mrs Waters in the village shop, and the people who now tend Lletherneuadd (Mr J. H. Phillips and family) for letting me look at the old homestead. Thanks to Annie, John, Ross and Trudy for valued insights into the story and my telling of it. Most importantly, Rebecca Nicolson and Aurea Carpenter of Short Books have been unfailingly patient, supportive and encouraging throughout. And so, as ever, has my husband, Robert. Thank you. Needless to say, any mistakes are the result of my own carelessness, exuberance and poor handwriting.

SEB

NOTE ON SOURCES

The main sources of reference for this book have been the newspaper reports of the time, but Dr John Cule's The Wreath on the Crown *(Gomerian Press, Llandyssul, 1967) is a masterly and detailed treatment of the story, which was never far from my side. An anonymous volume, published by D. Jones of Pencader in 1904 called* The Welsh Fasting Girl, *a complete history of the remarkable case of Sarah Jacob, and Robert Fowler's* A Complete History of the Welsh Fasting Girl *(Henry Redshaw, London, 1871) are the other principal sources. For background detail on Pencader and Llanfihangel-ar-arth I am indebted to Steve Dubé's book* This Small Corner *(Carmarthenshire County Council, 2000), an excellent example of what a local history should be.*

Siân Busby is a researcher and scriptwriter. She has worked in education, TV, film and theatre. She lives with her husband and two sons in London.